Ultimate Bankruptcy 2010

(Everything You Wanted to Know But Were Afraid to Ask)

By David Walden & Donald DiCarlo
http://www.bankruptcy101.us/

Table of Contents

E-Book Version Active Links

This Book Includes the E-Book Version Active Links in PDF format.

To get your copy of the Active Links enter the following URL into your search engine browser:

The Active Links begin on Page (11) at this location.

http://tinyurl.com/yye4xkn

Thank you for purchasing Ultimate Bankruptcy 2010 and watch for Ultimate Credit 2010 soon to follow.

Be sure to watch for our soon to be released "Ultimate Credit 2010".

This easy to follow credit restoration guide will show you how to get your good credit back in as little as six months after filing Chapter 7 Bankruptcy!

So stay tuned for more exciting information...

Introduction

It is critically important for anyone filing bankruptcy to understand that what your Bankruptcy ends up looking like, In every respect, is entirely up to you and you alone.

What I mean is that even the Chapter of Bankruptcy you end up filing, the amount of your plan payment (if you are filing under chapter 13), and ultimately what your life will look like during and after your bankruptcy is all up to you and you alone.

If your rely on your Bankruptcy Attorney to make your key bankruptcy decisions for you then you will most definitely be placing yourself at the mercy of the court and ultimately the banking and credit industry.

Bankruptcy Attorneys follow pre-determined guidelines provided by the Bankruptcy Court and will produce your Bankruptcy Petition according to what they know is the acceptable minimum standard that the trustee will allow.

What this means is that if you are filing Chapter 13 Bankruptcy, the information used to determine your Plan Payment will be based on guidelines alone and not what is in your best interest at all!

I recently did consulting work with one client who came to me because she felt her plan payments were making her life impossible and making her miserable as well!

She saw no possible way she could survive while fulfilling the requirements of her Chapter 13 Bankruptcy Plan Payment.

She had good reason to feel this way because when I sat down and analyzed her real world budget and what her plan payments were I was simply amazed.

Let's take a look at what she was strapped with to better understand what life can look like when left at the mercy of the Bankruptcy Attorney and Bankruptcy Court.

My client was strapped with a $784.00 Per WEEK Plan Payment that figures out to an annual payment of $40,768.00!

How could this happen to her when she had hired a Bankruptcy Attorney who was supposedly one of the "Best" in the area where she lived?

She was being forced to live at below poverty level and with no apparent benefit to her at all.

What happened here is that my client had done all of the necessary and minimum work that is required in order to fulfill what she believed were her only choices.

I immediately began working with her on completely revising her budget with a focus on maximizing benefits and minimizing loss then submitted it and got her plan payment reduced to $1,100.00 Per MONTH … Period!

That single act alone got her an incredible savings of $27,672.00 per year!

As with all things in life - the more you invest in anything - the more you will realize as a result!

More than ever before this is especially true with the Bankruptcy Process under the 2005 revisions; if you put in the minimum effort then you will get back minimum results!

The same can be said if you are in a situation where filing Chapter 7 Bankruptcy is in your best interest and you end up being forced into filing under Chapter 13 of the Bankruptcy Law.

The Bankruptcy Chapter that you end up having to file under is entirely up to you and the amount of effort you are willing to put into your case!

When you File Bankruptcy it is good to remember you are ultimately determining the quality of life for you and your family for up to five full years of the bankruptcy itself and then during the time following the bankruptcy as well.

For all of the reasons mentioned above, I want to start off by saying ATTITUDE when involved in the Bankruptcy filing process is crucial to how your experience will eventually play out.

If you are willing to approach your bankruptcy filing as though you are doing an investigation or doing research on the bankruptcy process then your experience will truly be an educational and positive one!

If you approach your bankruptcy filing as though it is a most horrible task you must do and something that you Hate doing … Then guess what your experience will no doubt be like?

As with all experiences in life … ATTITUDE is King!

Bankruptcy is BUSINESS and a Good Solid BUSINESS ATTITUDE is Imperative!

Ethics, Morality and the Law

Aside from attitude I want to add that following the rules as they are specified and applied in the bankruptcy court is crucial!

You need to make certain that with every action you take you are not doing anything that would be considered FRAUDULENT on any level by the bankruptcy court!

You need to tell your attorney everything and ask any and all questions to make certain that anything you are thinking about doing is acceptable to the court!

If you are thinking of selling a non-exempt piece of property prior to filing your bankruptcy, like a valuable coin collection or expensive antique furnishings, then it is extremely important to discuss this with your attorney.

Located at the link below is a video produced by the U.S. Bankruptcy court related to Bankruptcy Crime. I recommend that you pay close attention to what this video is saying and to heed its advice!

Under no circumstances would I ever advise you to lie or break any of the bankruptcy laws when preparing your case during the bankruptcy process! I recommend total compliance with all bankruptcy laws at all times!

Please Watch This Video:

Type the URL below into your Internet Browser:

http://tinyurl.com/ybxovtx

A FEW THINGS TO TAKE INTO ACCOUNT:

Please note that all recommended time frames mentioned in this publication are purposely set to be highly conservative.

When I say highly conservative, I am talking about recommending SIX MONTHS as opposed to the norm of 120 days or 90 days for taking actions related to assets and financial matters.

I am being very conservative in this publication because the last thing you or I want in your bankruptcy filing process is even one RED FLAG!

Before the changes in the bankruptcy law that took place in 2005, I would tell you to just find a good paralegal and file your bankruptcy pro-per/pro-se.

Now that the banking & creditor industry has gotten their agenda and changes made to the bankruptcy code, I would personally never consider filing any chapter of bankruptcy without the representation of a good attorney!

I say this because the changes that were made in the bankruptcy law were done by the Credit Card and Banking Industry and the attitude of the Bankruptcy Court seems to have changed to a more aggressive and pro-creditor position.

I would never want to give the credit card or banking industry the upper hand with my post bankruptcy life. These two industries have perpetrated a terrible crime against the American People with this new bankruptcy law! The creditor and banking industry spent millions of dollars through their lobbyists to bribe Our Congress and get this travesty of a new bankruptcy law passed!

Special Notices

NOTICE #1 PRINT OUT THE LAST (7) PAGES OF THIS BOOK and refer to them regularly throughout the Planning Stages of your Bankruptcy.

In fact, refer to these tools right up to the time of your actually filing your bankruptcy.

NOTICE #2 EMERGENCY BANKRUPTCY FILING: If you are in a situation where you have a Pending Foreclosure Sale about to take place on your home – even if only a day or so away – then you will need to file what is known as an "EMERGENCY BANKRUPTCY FILING" and this single act will stop the Foreclosure Sale in its tracks!

If this is the case you need to get an appointment with a local bankruptcy attorney immediately! Any Bankruptcy Attorney will know what to do in order to file an Emergency Bankruptcy petition on your behalf.

If you cannot get an appointment with an attorney then contact a paralegal service in your area and they should know what to do.

If you use this alternative then you will need to immediately make an appointment with a bankruptcy attorney to complete the paperwork A.S.A.P or your Emergency Filing will be tossed!

NOTICE #3 BANKRUPTCY ATTORNEYS: For what ever reason Bankruptcy Attorneys can be overwhelmed with work or simply be ultimate procrastinators.

THERE MAY BE TIMES WHEN YOU NEED TO PLACE DEMANDS ON YOUR ATTORNEY DUE TO ACTIONS ORDERED BY THE BANKRUPTCY COURT THAT MUST BE TAKEN ON YOUR BEHALF!

Do not allow yourself to be walked on by the person you are paying to represent you with your bankruptcy! Remember to be civil with your attorney at all times but also remember to be firm and assert yourself if necessary!

Do not feel intimidated because your attorney is schooled in the legal process and you are only the client. It is because you are the client and have paid your attorney for legal representation that your attorney works for you and not the other way around!

If you do not understand something have your attorney explain in a manner that you can understand.

Make certain that you find an attorney who returns telephone calls and does not hide from their clients

NOTICE #4 MEANS TEST: You will need to deal with the newly added "MEANS TEST" resulting from changed made to the Bankruptcy Code in 2005.

Note: There is No "Means Test" required if you are a "Business Debtor"

If one half or more of your indebtedness is business related, then you are considered a business debtor and you are not required to take and pass the "means test"

If over half of your indebtedness is consumer and not business related debt, then you will need to take and pass the "means test".

The "Means Test" for consumer debtors

The "Means Test" came into being as a result of the revision of the Bankruptcy Laws in 2005 with the help of Joseph Biden.

This "Test" is another way to maneuver consumers into having to file for Chapter 13 instead of Chapter 7 to give the Bank & Creditor Industry even more of your hard earned money and indentured servitude!

I feel that the best way for you to deal with the "Means Test" element of your bankruptcy filing is to FIRST determine which chapter is right for you!

11

This should come naturally to you once you have completed your minimum of (3) FREE Legal Consultations with qualified Bankruptcy Attorneys.

If you have asked all of the right questions and have made certain to understand the answers, you should now be somewhat prepared.

What you need to do next is study the "Means Test" requirement related to the Chapter of Bankruptcy you wish to file.

Study the guidelines to see who is able to qualify for the Bankruptcy Chapter you determine is best for you to file under.

One major issue involving the "Means Test" is the Income Factor.

According to the new Bankruptcy Law, your net income cannot exceed the "state Median income" for the state where you are filing by more than 25% or you will be forced to file under the Chapter 13 Bankruptcy Code!

Median Income by State – Click below:

http://www.usdoj.gov/ust/eo/bapcpa/20090315/bci_data/median_incom e_table.htm

The Median Income issue is not an impossible hurdle to overcome. With some creative thinking and flexibility related to your current job situation you can deal with this successfully.

If you feel the outcome is worthwhile then you will be able to get around this income issue without too much grief.

What getting past this "Median Income" requirement has meant for many people is to actually take on a new source of employment where the income will not stop them from filing under chapter 7 if that is their objective.

What this has meant for others is that the spouse with the highest income has ended up quitting their job for a few months until their Chapter 7 Bankruptcy has been completed and all debt has been discharged.

Of course the benefits gained by the end result should dictate what decision you will make regarding your own situation and how you will deal with the "Median Income" requirement

Once you have gotten by the "Median Income" Issue of the "Means Test" then you need to address your Income to Debt Ratio which can best be done by down loading and printing work copies of Schedules I & J.

Once you have done this you can get your numbers close to where they need to be in order to file the chapter you desire.

Once you think you have gotten pretty close then go to the "Means Test" page and apply those numbers there!

Schedule I – Current Income Statement

http://www.uscourts.gov/rules/BK_Forms_1207/B_006I_1207f.pdf

Schedule J – Current Expenditures

http://www.uscourts.gov/rules/BK_Forms_1207/B_006J_1207f.pdf

Remember that in order to quality for Chapter 7 Bankruptcy your total cost of expenditures when subtracted from your total combined income must equal no more than $15.00 left over or on the plus side!

If you have even $25.00 on the plus side in today's world you could be raising a red flag with the Chapter 7 Bankruptcy Trustee who will try to get most everyone filing into a Chapter 13 Bankruptcy!

For Chapter 7 Bankruptcy – Follow These (3) Steps:

STEP 1:

Complete Schedules I & J and see if your total cost of expenditures/cost of living when subtracted from your total combined income results in no more than $15.00 or so left on the plus side!

Schedule I – Current Income Statement

http://www.uscourts.gov/rules/BK_Forms_1207/B_006I_1207f.pdf

Schedule J – Current Expenditures

http://www.uscourts.gov/rules/BK_Forms_1207/B_006J_1207f.pdf

Once you have completed this step and the numbers work for you confirm that the amounts you have shown for your cost of living are acceptable to the Chapter 7 Bankruptcy Trustee.

STEP 2:

Next, complete the "Means Test" and make certain that the result is in complete agreement with your Schedule I & J so you still qualify under the "Median Income" Requirement.

STEP 3:

Do not become intimidated by all of this … what it means is that you simply need to complete Step 1 and make the numbers work out with the numbers that will qualify you for Chapter 7 Bankruptcy.

You need to make certain that your cost of living claims are reasonable and are acceptable with the Chapter 7 Bankruptcy Trustee and this is something that your Bankruptcy Attorney can work with you on. (be assertive where you feel you must)

For Chapter 13 Bankruptcy:

When Schedules I & J are completed for Ch. 7 Bankruptcy and total expenditures/cost of living are subtracted from total combined income then the approximate amount left on the plus side will represent what your Monthly Plan Payment will look like!

Pay close to the story at the beginning of this publication because you can avoid severe monthly plan payments by doing your homework here and making certain that all of your living expenses are adequately covered and represented on your expenditures statement.

When you have completed your "Means Test" preparation work by adjusting the info on schedules I & J then go directly to the on line "means test" and see if there are any issues you still need to deal with.

Remember to plug into the "Means Test" only after you have done your work with Schedules I & J linked above.

When you feel you are close to where you need to be with your income to debt ratio (in order to file the Chapter of Bankruptcy that works best for you) you can discuss how to move forward with your Bankruptcy Attorney.

If you are having difficulty with this issue then you need to consult your Bankruptcy Attorney for advice and assistance.

Form B22A can be found by clicking here! (used to calculate means test for chapter 7)

Form B22C can be found by clicking here! (used to calculate means test for chapter 13)

It is imperative that you make your greatest efforts right here because this is one of the critical points of CONTROL for you plan.

You need to remember that every issue in the world can be resolved with the proper approach and attitude and a bit of creativity and ingenuity!

A critical part of the "means test" is where you compare your current income amount with the median income for the state where you reside. For this reason the state where you reside will most definitely have an impact on your strategy.

If after completing your "means test" you do not qualify for filing a Chapter 7 Bankruptcy because your income is still too high and Chapter 7 is what your plan calls for then you need to go back to the drawing board and revise your Schedules I & J until the numbers work!

If your income is the main issue here you may need to make changes to your employment situation to make your plan work. If that is not a realistic option perhaps you need to buy or lease a new vehicle that will give you payments that will adjust your schedules as needed.

These are the best two areas for adjusting your schedules because you cannot do much to modify your income other than taking less hours or taking another job altogether or perhaps having your spouse quit their job.

I believe the best way to work with adjusting your schedules I & J is to have them printed out and work from the print out. This way you can make notes on what changes you are making and make certain to document all of the adjustments for future reference.

In this way you will understand what adjustments you made even a month or so from today.

Just remember these two guidelines:

If you want to file for Chapter 7 Bankruptcy then your income to debt ratio should come out close to even. So if your income is $1,700 per month your cost of living should be about $1,700 per month.

If you want to file for Chapter 13 Bankruptcy then your income to debt ratio should come out positive by the amount you will need in your bankruptcy plan.

So if you are filing a chapter 13 because you have an arrearage on your home of say $10,000 and it is to be paid out over (5) years, then your income needs to be $1,875 or $1,700 + $175.00 = 1,875 with your cost of living at $1700 per month.

The cost of living in this case would amount to all items listed on you Schedule J that includes any mortgages, car payments, your chapter 13 plan payment and all other items listed.

The reason for the additional income is that the $10,000 arrears amount is as follows:

5 yrs = 60 months (5 yr plan=5 at 12 months per yr = 60 months)

5 yrs = 260 weeks (5 yrs x 52 weeks = 260 weeks total)

10,000 divided by 260 weeks = 38.46 per week

So $38.46 x 52 weeks = $1,999.92 per year divided by 12 months = $166.66 so figure that $175.00 per month should also cover bankruptcy fees figured in.

So in this case you needed an additional $175.00 per month added to your income should work out pretty close. Once you have a figure that you think meets your plan then you need to discuss this figure with your Bankruptcy Attorney.

Your income before was $1,700 plus $175.00 per month for your plan payment = $1,875 per month income. (1,700 + 175 = 1,875 per month)

Remember that your Bankruptcy Attorney is there to help you with this process and that this is just offered as a general guideline for making your schedules and budget work.

This can serve as your formula for dealing with the income to debt ratio part of your "Means Test" requirement.

It is amazing that Our U.S. Congress who are supposed to be serving the best interests of their constituency, the American People, and the best interests of our nation as a whole, would instead give preference to taking Bribery Money from the Credit Card Industry who are the perpetrators who paid them off through their lobbyists … Then turned around in the past two years and absconded with over 13 trillion dollars of our tax payer money!

http://www.democracynow.org/2009/6/22/report_goldman_sachs_on_pace_to

http://www.democracynow.org/2008/11/17/naomi_klein_on_the_bailout_profiteers

NOTE: For a brief look at recent history:

MBNA was one of the prime movers in lobbying for the passage of the Bankruptcy Abuse Prevention and Consumer Protection Act of 2005, which took 11 years and **millions of dollars spent on lobbying before the act was finally passed** when 15 Democrats (all of whom had received campaign contributions from MBNA, notably Joseph R. Biden, Jr. (D-DE) $147,700) joined with their Republican colleagues to
sign it into law.[*citation needed*] (This Informatin taken from Wikipedia on line)

Acquiring All Information You Need

I have this friend Steve who has been a really good friend of mine over the past twelve years. Steve found himself in a very difficult financial position a few years back.

Steve is married with (3) kids who were at the time in their teens and all approaching adulthood. It seemed that things were going along well with Steve and his family at least up until that time.

Then suddenly it happened! Steve's wife became ill and had to be rushed to the hospital.

It was August 2004 and Steve's wife had become very ill with what I thought was a very minor problem, appendicitis, and she had to be rushed to the hospital by ambulance for emergency surgery. If that wasn't upsetting enough during that same period Steve also lost his job.

Ok, this is a tough situation for anyone to cope with for sure but none of that was as traumatic as when the hospital bill arrived in the mail a few weeks later!

I had been running my bankruptcy service for about seven years at this point so the day when the medical bill arrived, Steve ended up calling me in a panic.

He asked me to guess what the hospital bill had come out to for his wife's surgery and one week stay in the hospital? I said oh for an appendicitis attack and related surgery probably around $30,000.00 (I was trying to be conservative). Steve said "I wish … guess again" So I guessed $50,000.00 the next time. "No he said … guess again" So I guessed $70,000.00!

Wrong Again …"The bill alone came to over $120,000.00 plus other incidentals! Steve was very upset and asking me where in the hell he is supposed to come up with that kind of money?

Well, I could not believe the charges that the hospital came up with, I mean this is an appendicitis attack and related hospitalization, not for a brain surgery operation!

So, what could I say to Steve other than to suggest that he and his wife come in for a bankruptcy consultation?   I told him that due to his unemployment circumstances and Income to debt ratio that I was pretty sure he could file for chapter 7 bankruptcy.

That is precisely what he did. So much stress and worry about his wife's illness and his losing his job plus the hospital bill hanging over their heads like a noose!

Now on top of that even more stress was beginning to pile up due to Steve's job loss situation and with the creditors who were starting to swarm.

The calls started coming in from the bill collectors who could not have cared less about his story and what happened to he and his wife and family!

Soon enough there would be so much creditor harassment and so many sleepless nights that all Steve could do is worry about how he and his family were going to survive this catastrophe?

Steve was far more lucky than anyone in a similar financial situation today because Steve was able to file his bankruptcy under the pre-2005 bankruptcy law!

Today so much has changed for the struggling consumer. The new bankruptcy code has been designed to serve the desires and greed of the banking and credit industry.

It is by no accident that we can thank the credit and banking industry for bribing OUR Congressmen through their lobbyists in order to get the changes in the bankruptcy law that they wanted.

The new bankruptcy code has been designed to give the shaft to the consumer … Hey … That's You and Me … in every way that is possible!

If you have found yourself in similar financial circumstances with your financial life then one of the first things you need to do is to take every means available to you to protect yourself.

You need to work hard to make sure that you and your family are not further victims of the banking and creditor industry.

You need to not let yourself be shafted by the new bankruptcy law and further shafted by the credit and banking industry who created it!

First off you need to locate a reliable and reasonably priced Bankruptcy Attorney in your general area.

Be certain that you find an attorney who specializes in bankruptcy and is very experienced in the bankruptcy court and one who truly knows the bankruptcy law!

Below I am outlining the best possible way for you to find a Bankruptcy Attorney in your area that you can truly rely on and more importantly an attorney who you feel comfortable working with.

How to find a reliable and responsible Attorney?

When looking for a competent bankruptcy attorney there are a number of things you can do to make certain that you have the best in your area for the money you will be charged.

Doing a good job here will assure you that your bankruptcy hearing goes smoothly and without any snags or hitches!

Also, be sure to take pen and notebook with you to all of your consultations and to take notes on everything the attorney says related to your specific case.

Remember to ask questions on what is allowed and not allowed by the bankruptcy court related to your personal property and your payment history and all. (See my questions list in the last section of this publication)

Remember to cover all of the basic info related to exemptions and reaffirming debt and the rules as they apply to you and your specific situation.

Below is a guideline for identifying the best attorney for filing your bankruptcy with while learning everything you need to know prior to your filing.

1. Make appointments with local attorneys for at least (3) Free Bankruptcy Consultations.

   It is important that you have these free consultations in order to gain a good understanding of how the bankruptcy process actually works.

   Go in equipped with a list of every Question that you can think of or bring the list I provided here and add to that list. Remember that in the world of bankruptcy as it is currently practiced there is no such thing as a dumb question!

   During each consultation it is important that you ask any and all questions you may have previously missed or to clarify ones that you did not understand the attorney's explanation of in the past.

   Keep asking these questions until the answers are clear in your mind. In this way you will cover most everything prior to your actually filing.

   By the time you experience your third consultation you will have a good basic knowledge regarding the bankruptcy filing process and related rules. You will be able to ask even more in depth questions like clarifying the difference between Chapter 7 & Chapter 13 bankruptcy and which chapter is best for you?

Now you will be able to better understand pretty much how it all works and reduce any stress you may have had.

Most importantly you will have a pretty clear idea of which attorney knows their stuff better than the rest and seems most reliable!

Once you have completed your third consultation you will need to sit down with your spouse or significant other(s) and together you can determine which attorney seemed most competent and knowledgeable.

It will also be important to identify which of the attorneys you feel most comfortable working with so that there are no personality conflicts of any kind here.

Please note that there actually are attorneys out there who will really scold you and try to make you feel terrible and guilty! I believe that this type of attorney is simply trying to intimidate their potential client so that they can get them to pay even higher attorney fees!

If you come across one of these jokers I believe it is best to just blow them off! So, just move on. This kind of attorney is a pathetic being and should not be practicing law at all!

2. Visit local bankruptcy or social service organizations in your area to see if they know which Bankruptcy Attorneys seem to have the least amount of complaints or is the most liked for the service they provide.

3. Ask friends and associates if they know anyone who ever filed for bankruptcy and who really liked the service they received from their attorney. (This can be a problem since filing for bankruptcy can be a very embarrassing experience for some … but if you are comfortable with it … and the person you are asking is not a co-worker or job related acquaintance then hey … Ask!)

4. Contact your local Better Business Bureau or Bar Association and check for local Bankruptcy Attorney' ratings … just ask.

5. Contact local paralegal services that offer bankruptcy filing as a part of their services. (Make sure you do this step only After you have had all of your Bankruptcy Attorney consultations.

   It is imperative that you visit your local attorneys first in order to have all of your questions answered and to learn all of the basics and rules/red flag areas prior to filing.)

   In this way you will already have a general knowledge and be in a better place to make a decision regarding the use of a paralegal service. (Remember that paralegals cannot answer questions related to bankruptcy law and so you must get this information from your local bankruptcy attorney)

   Note: Because Paralegals are not licensed attorney's they are not allowed to answer questions of any kind that could be interpreted as legal in nature.

6. Contact your legal aide organization(s) in your area and see if they are willing to recommend anyone.

7. Visit bankruptcy hearings at your local bankruptcy court and see which attorney's appear to have the least amount of difficulty with their client filings. (You can find out hearing times by contacting your local bankruptcy court.)

   What you will need to know about the state where you reside and how that relates to your bankruptcy filing.

   You can also learn more about this topic during your Free Bankruptcy Consultations with attorneys in your general area. You can ask the attorney if it may be better for you to use the federal or state exemptions also.

   Are people who file for bankruptcy really bad or evil people who should have known better and should feel guilty for getting themselves into their financial situation they are in now?

   Perhaps what we really need to be asking is the question who exactly is responsible for so many Americans having to file for bankruptcy in the first place?

There are a number of factors we need to consider here.

In my eleven plus years of working as a bankruptcy specialist I found the following:

The number one reason people were forced to file for bankruptcy was medical expenses! Just one hospitalization of one of the children or a spouse member would do it!

The number two reason was loss of job of either spouse.

The number three reason was divorce! (A lot of the time the third reason resulted from the existence of the first two!)

The fact is that the U.S. Banking Industry has pretty much acted criminally and they have absconded with more than 13 Trillion Dollars of Our Tax Dollars!

The Banking Executives stole all of this money after creating the financial mess that every American is struggling with today!

Most of this mess was driven by the unbridled GREED of so many irresponsible Con Artists in high positions in the banking industry!

Should you feel guilty about being a victim of their greed driven behavior … NO … ABSOLUTELY NOT!

If you are still unconvinced regarding this matter then please click on this link below and watch the interview with Michael Moore regarding his latest movie release:

http://www.democracynow.org/2009/9/24/after_20_years_of_film_making_on

We are all dependent upon our government to protect us and to act responsibly when special interests are acting irresponsibly.

If our government is allowing our tax dollars to be stolen right out from under us then I guess the big question we need to be asking is this; Do B of A or their C.E.O.'s feel guilty about what they have done? Do AIG and their C.E.O.'s feel guilty? Do Chase and their C.E.O.'s feel guilty? Should any of us feel guilty under the current situation as it is being played out today?

In all of my eleven plus years of working as a bankruptcy specialist in CA, I can remember only one person who I felt was actually trying to cheat the system!

Other than that one case among the thousands of others … all of the rest were people having to file for bankruptcy because of job loss or health problems or hospitalizations or a bad divorce or some other kind of personal catastrophe!

A Few Questions You May Need To Consider Asking:

Which Chapter of bankruptcy is best for me to file in my current situation?

Do I have a choice as to which chapter of bankruptcy I can file?

Would Chapter 7 or Chapter 13 bankruptcy be the best Chapter for me to file in order to protect most or all of my assets?

If I am self-employed can I still file either Ch. 7 or Ch. 13 bankruptcy or do I have to file Ch. 13 only?

If I am 1099 or Contract laborer can I still file either Ch. 7 or Ch. 13 Bankruptcy?

If I file Ch. 7 bankruptcy can I still keep my home?

If I file for Ch. 7 bankruptcy can I reaffirm my home loan debt(s) and be able to keep my home or will I be forced to file for Ch. 13 bankruptcy?

If I do keep my home will I lose any of my equity position?

If I keep my home will I have to continue making my mortgage payments as usual?

Can I get rid of my house as part of my bankruptcy filing and do so without penalty?

If I choose to surrender my home will I have to repay any of my financing as part of the bankruptcy?

Will my bankruptcy get rid of both my 1st and 2nd mortgages or will I have to pay either of them back even after filing bankruptcy?

Can I keep my car as a part of my bankruptcy filing?

Will my car qualify for exemption based upon its equity value?

Can I buy a new car before filing for bankruptcy and keep the car even though I am filing for bankruptcy?

If my car does qualify for exemption can I keep my Car without penalty?

Can I get rid of my car and car payment without penalty?

If I give up my car and car payment will it hurt my chance for filing Ch 7 bankruptcy because of the impact on my budget?

Am I allowed to have income and/or cash when filing for bankruptcy?

If I am allowed to have income and/or cash in my possession then how much can I have that will not be placed in jeopardy?

Will I get into any trouble with my employer for filing bankruptcy?

Can my employer legally fire me because I have filed for bankruptcy?

Can I be legally kept from being hired on a job especially if my work has any kind of security clearance related to it because of my filing for bankruptcy?

Am I breaking the law when filing for bankruptcy?

The reality is that by filing for bankruptcy you are actually doing the responsible thing.

If you have no way of paying your creditors or arranging for terms that are workable for you then by doing nothing you are actually acting irresponsibly.

What do I need to know when putting together my personal information for the bankruptcy petition?

How critical is the Budget part of my bankruptcy petition?

How do I determine real world figures for my living expenses?

Who should I pay off prior to filing for bankruptcy?

Can I legally pay off debt to friends and family prior to filing for bankruptcy?

What can I legally keep other than my car and my house?

Can I keep coin collections or antique furniture or family heirlooms or other value property when filing for bankruptcy?

What happens to my IRS Debt?

How does the bankruptcy law treat IRS debt and what are my requirements in order to be able to liquidate my IRS debt as a part of my bankruptcy filing?

Are there any conditions related to IRS debt that I need to know in order to have my IRS debt liquidated through bankruptcy?

What happens to my School Loans as a result of my filing for bankruptcy?

Are my school loans eliminated as a result of my filing for bankruptcy?

Can filing for bankruptcy help me to deal with my school loan payments that are prohibitively high?

What happens to my Credit Card Debt?

Will I have to pay back any of my credit card debt?

Is there any credit card debt that I should consider reaffirming?

What happens to my Debt to friends and family?

Can I pay back my good friend Tom who I borrowed $1,500.00 from prior to filing my bankruptcy?

Can I pay back Aunt Bea who I borrowed money from last year?

Who should I file against on my bankruptcy petition?

> Can I choose to not file bankruptcy against certain creditors who I owe money too because I really like having their Visa or MasterCard?

> Can I choose to not file bankruptcy against my friends and family who I have outstanding debts with?

Is it ok to withhold financial information from the bankruptcy court?

> It is in your best interest to realize that the bankruptcy court is a federal court and the bankruptcy laws are federal laws …enough said?

What happens to my Gambling Debt?

> What happens if I have gambling debt with various casino's where I play?

OTHER QUESTIONS YOU MAY WANT TO ASK:

What if I have Collection Accounts?

How will I be protected from creditors by filing bankruptcy?

Do I need to have an Attorney in order to file for bankruptcy?

Can I go out and buy a new car prior to filing for bankruptcy?

Can I hide personal property and just not report it to the bankruptcy court in my petition paperwork?

Can I give my car or other personal property away to others to hold for me prior to filing for bankruptcy?

Can I sell my personal property to friends or family prior to filing for bankruptcy?

Can I sell and buy things if they are all done with CASH only?

Planning Your Bankruptcy

The best way to assure that you achieve the outcome that you want is to plan your bankruptcy well in advance.

The key to being successful with your plan is to appear as though nothing at all was ever planned!

I WANT TO REPEAT THIS POINT IN ORDER TO MAKE IT CRYSTAL CLEAR & NOT MISSED!

It is important that your bankruptcy DOES NOT APPEAR TO BE PRE-PLANNED ON ANY LEVEL OR IN ANY WAY AND THIS WILL AVOID ANY RED FLAGS THAT COULD RESULT!

One way to remove the appearance of having planned your bankruptcy is to complete all necessary actions AT LEAST SIX MONTHS IN ADVANCE!

If you feel this is impossible or next to impossible due to pressures being placed on you by hungry creditors and collection agencies, then drop down to the section entitled **"Watch the Timing!"**

Your bankruptcy, as with any other financial business matter, needs to be planned out well in advance of your actual filing!

For this reason it is critical that you have followed through with all of the steps outlined in the FREE publication I sent you. In this way you will now have a good sense of all of the rules and hence have some idea of what you need to do in order to get the result you want.

When and how you approach the filing of your bankruptcy will determine just how much you and you family will benefit as a result.

You can take a process that is for most people a totally "negative" one involving extreme stress and long term struggle and misery and turn it into a blessing.

When working with many if not most of my bankruptcy clients from the past, the experience for them was a total admission of failure, defeat and guilt!

Part of my job at the time was to help my clients realize that they were clearly as much victims of the banking and credit industry as they were responsible for their financial situation.

What was being done to them was far beyond anything they had ever done themselves to end up in their desperate situations.   If anything, that situation is even more prominent today!

The actual reality is that this capitalist system has been designed in such a way as to always have a certain percentage of the population failing at all times! The system requires a certain level of unemployment to exist at all times. (This topic is an entirely different matter for another place and time)

In contrast to the negative failure model that most experience in this process, you can turn your bankruptcy experience into a positive life changing event.

You can turn your bankruptcy filing into a truly productive event with minimal effort and planning. You can turn what can be a truly "negative" experience for many into a positive and beneficial step forward in your financial life and with little or no struggle or misery at all.

What's more you can do all of this with minimal stress as well.
When you think about it, most of our stress comes from our NOT KNOWING the future and fear related to not knowing what might result.

The best way to rid ourselves of FEAR is through learning everything you can about your situation and taking control of the process you are involved in. The end result is that you control the process and you eliminate your fear(s).

As with most things in our lifetime ATTITUDE can matter more than anything else.

When you are contemplating bankruptcy you can emulate the struggling loser who is overcome with guilt and feelings of failure … or you can

33

emulate the big corporation that is moving forward and assuring that they will lose little or nothing and come out smelling like a rose!

A big part of how your bankruptcy experience will turn out will be determined by your ATTITUDE regarding the bankruptcy process itself!

Do you remember when Pan Am Airlines filed for bankruptcy?

http://tinyurl.com/yerqzll

I can assure you that the management at Pan Am and Eastern Airlines worked diligently in preparing for their bankruptcy.

You can be certain that a whole battery of attorneys was put into place to protect every one of their valued assets and their corporate position at all costs as a part of their bankruptcy filing!

You can be assured that Pan Am & Eastern Airlines planned every move in advance and knew all of the options available to them before they even started.

No doubt they did everything in their power to come out of this bankruptcy as lean and clean as they could and with all of the benefits that would result maximized to the highest level possible!

If you look at how the corporate world utilizes this process you can be sure that their results are defined as a bottom line financial affair. In other words they do not personalize any part of this process.

It is just business as usual and the bankruptcy is a strategic maneuver to assure financial survival with a minimum of loss.

It is this same approach that we are going to use with my "Bankruptcy Control System" to assure that every person filing approaches their bankruptcy as a business matter and nothing less!

You need to plan every move you make to guarantee that you will experience minimum loss and maximum gain with your strategy … just like Pan Am and Eastern Airlines did.

YOU NEED TO EMULATE THE CORPORATE MODEL WHEN FILING YOUR BANKRUPTCY AND THINK JUST LIKE THE BANKS AND THE CREDITOR INDUSTRY AND LIKE ALL CORPORATIONS DO!

Considering all that has happened here in the U.S. over the past eight years it seems pretty clear that the best approach might very well be to simply let the corporate model be your guide!

Taking Control - The Bankruptcy Control System

A major element I want to discuss in this section relates to another key element of your Bankruptcy Filing.

By utilizing my Bankruptcy Control System you will be directly involved in the design of key elements of your bankruptcy petition and especially your budget statement!

On my webpage I frequently mentioned the importance of using my "Bankruptcy Control System" in order to achieve your ultimate goals when preparing your bankruptcy petition.

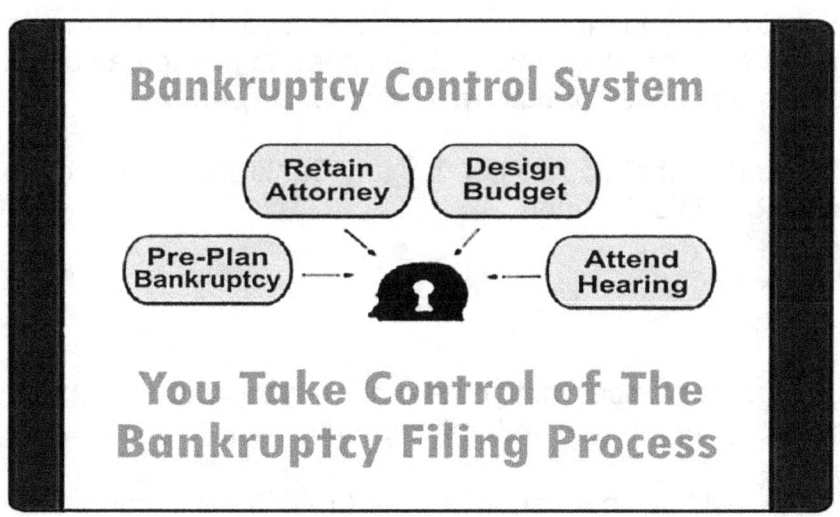

By using my "Bankruptcy Control System" you will make your bankruptcy filing straight forward and most beneficial to you rather than the creditors who have created most of the financial mess we all have to deal with today.

My Bankruptcy Control System is composed of (4) distinct areas that are listed in the order they need to be completed:

1) Securing information from a Bankruptcy Attorney in a Nearby Community to learn everything possible prior to planning out your bankruptcy.

   WARNING: Do Not Pay Any Fees To Any Bankruptcy Attorney For Any Reason at this time or Until you have done all of your pre-planning work and are actually ready to begin the filing process!

   At this time You Are Not Ready to Document anything related to bankruptcy or that you are even thinking about filing for bankruptcy.

   Bankruptcy Information gathered in advance of your filing could be used against you by unscrupulous creditors if they feel they can document any intent on your part!

   For instance, you may not be certain that you will be filing bankruptcy and have charge accounts that you need to use to pay bills or make clothing purchases or auto repairs or for any reason.

   Make certain that you do not pay any Bankruptcy Attorney for anything at this time and

   NEVER TELL A CREDITOR THAT YOU ARE THINKING ABOUT FILING BANKRUPTCY!

   You must remember that you are only on the information gathering phase of your journey and nothing more.

   Also, I would act innocent with your Free Consultation attorney's and would make certain that they do not know anything about what you are planning or preparing so that they cannot in any way damage your position.

2) Use the information you have gathered from all of your Free Attorney Consultations for Pre-Planning Your Bankruptcy Filing and Developing a solid plan for achieving the outcomes that you have prioritized.

3) Locate and RETAIN/PAY a Local Attorney who is both Reputable and Accessible, yet trustworthy. Choose an attorney with whom you feel comfortable working and pay/retain them for your bankruptcy representation.

   Remember to choose someone who you feel comfortable working with and where there are no personality conflicts.

4) Begin Fine Tuning your Budget (for schedules I & J) taking into account your "means test" information as well. Make certain to do this with oversight from your Bankruptcy Attorney and begin working through the budget preparation process.

Schedule I – Current Income Statement

http://www.uscourts.gov/rules/BK_Forms_1207/B_006I_1207f.pdf

Schedule J – Current Expenditures

http://www.uscourts.gov/rules/BK_Forms_1207/B_006J_1207f.pdf

Notice how the form states "CURRENT" before each of these statements. When dealing with bankruptcy information the numbers you will use are "here and now" figures and not "what you think you will" or "what you used to" but these are your "CURRENT" figures.

PLEASE AVOID MAKING ANY ASSUMPTIONS DURING THIS PROCESS!

Use of Checklist (Basic Outline of Procedures)

In order to make certain that you do not miss one single element of Planning your Bankruptcy and implementing your Plan it is imperative that you use the "Bankruptcy Checklist" included in this publication!

The "Bankruptcy Checklist" begins on **Page 100** at the end of this publication and NEEDS TO BE PRINTED OUT WHEN YOU BEGIN THIS PROCESS!

Always Be Prepared with your statements and contracts ...

You will need to supply your bankruptcy attorney with all relevant information for you bankruptcy petition.

That means you will need to supply a number of things including but not limited to:

- Latest copy of each of your unsecured creditor statements
- Copies of all of your collection accounts with collection agencies (it is best to staple the collection notice to the original creditor statement)
- Copies of all of your secured bills including mortgage and/or auto loans
- Copies of any relevant IRS notices or statements payment plans, etc
- Copies of any outstanding school loans
- Copies of any judgments or liens or info related to repossessions
- Copies of paycheck stubs
- Copies of any liens on your home
- Copies of all medical and hospital bills
- Copies of any recent bills of sale

The above list will give you some idea of what your Bankruptcy Attorney will need from you. Your attorney will give you their list of what they want and the manner they want you to submit it to them.

Pre-Planning Your Bankruptcy Filing

I have known several people who made certain to plan out their bankruptcy experience in every detail and would not think of doing it any other way.

Below is the advice that was shared with me by many who have planned out and filed their petition with incredible success.

Begin by making a list of all of your assets you want to protect.

Then determine just how much money (cash) you want to have on hand for your new start after your bankruptcy.

Determine what secured property(s) you want to keep and make plans to reaffirm the debt(s) that secure(s) that property.

You will want to decide if it is best to reaffirm your mortgage on your home or if it is too upside down and you prefer to surrender it.

You will need to remember that the whole purpose of filing your bankruptcy is to give you and your family a new start!

The key to making this work effectively is to make your life pretty much debt free after your bankruptcy.

The last thing you will want when moving forward for your life after bankruptcy is the anchor of a home that has no real equity value and will lock you into negative mortgage payments for a very long time.

I do not recommend trying to save a home that is clearly upside down and of no real value to you after bankruptcy.

Remember that the housing market is very depressed today and you can get a great deal on a replacement home at a great price.

If you choose to create a new credit profile after filing your bankruptcy you can use my soon to be released publication "Ultimate Credit 2010" or 'How to Have Your Good Credit Back Just Six Months After Bankruptcy' and you will be able to purchase another home in less than a year!

In this real estate market you can get into another home that is nicer than your current one but now less expensive as well because of the real estate market.

(If you currently own your home, you will want to look at real world market value and the resulting amount of equity you currently have. You need to base your decision to reaffirm or surrender on true equity value position. Your decision needs to be made as a sound business decision based on actual dollar value.)

You are now at the stage of pre-planning your bankruptcy where the most crucial choices will be made and will be directly related to what chapter of bankruptcy you will be permitted to file or what chapter is the most beneficial for you to file under!

Please understand that one of the main purposes of pre-planning your bankruptcy is to pre-design your future after bankruptcy by setting into motion key decisions that will determine what chapter you will file.

If, for instance you have too much income and are planning to file bankruptcy under the Chapter 7 bankruptcy code you will need to take certain actions now.

In order to file for chapter 7 you may need to alter your budget figures so that your cost of living is increased or your income is decreased.

What many have done to increase their monthly expenses is to go out and purchase or lease a new car!

By purchasing a new car they are also guaranteeing that they will have reliable transportation once they have filed their bankruptcy.

The ideal amount for the new car payment can be determined by knowing just how much the expense statement needed to be adjusted upward.

By making a new car purchase the cost of living figure can be raised by $400.00 per month and more!

Making a purchase like this is also a way of protecting your future life style by making certain that you have a highly reliable car with a solid factory warranty.

Having a new car can prevent expensive auto repair bills and remove any worry about getting to work late because the car has "broken down again".

Making such a move also guarantees safety for the entire family when traveling on long trips or just running around town.

Remember you will be reaffirming this debt which means you WILL NOT be filing bankruptcy on this auto loan or auto lease! YOU WILL BE REAFFIRMING THIS DEBT AND PAYING IT WITHOUT INTERRUPTION. DISCUSS WITH YOUR BANKRUPTCY ATTORNEY!

Also, remember that you will be re-establishing your credit with this purchase … ALWAYS BE ON TIME OR EARLY WITH YOUR PAYMENT AND NEVER LATE WITH THIS CREDITOR!

You must know that you can afford the car payment that you are establishing with this purchase!

ALWAYS DISCUSS YOUR PLANS WITH YOUR ATTORNEY PRIOR TO TAKING ANY ACTION!

Considering that you are not supposed to have decent credit for at least (10) years after filling for bankruptcy this auto purchase is a logical decision to make because you will be creating a positive credit history with this new car loan.

If things were to happen according to what the creditors want you would not be able to have good credit to purchase another car for at least (10) years so this is a good time to do so now before you file your bankruptcy!

Please understand that it is critically important that you have had all of your Free Bankruptcy Consultations with reputable bankruptcy attorneys before starting this pre-planning process!

You will soon learn that the key element in the bankruptcy filing process is your income to debt ratio as defined by your budget!

You must know in advance of hiring your attorney how to manipulate this budget to the end that you desire. This is a big part of what your pre-planning is all about.

It is imperative that you know the bankruptcy rules of engagement so that you can know how to deal with your pre-planning and how to create the kind of budget that will serve you well.

As you will soon realize it is your budget where you will be able to have the most impact on how your bankruptcy will play out.

Insider Tricks of the Trade

The consensus is that "one key to being successful with your bankruptcy plan is to create the appearance that no part of it was ever planned at all!"

The best way to achieve an unplanned appearance is to do things well in advance of your ever filing for bankruptcy. A good rule of thumb is to take all actions at least SIX MONTHS prior to your filing.

Also, one thing you never want to do in the course of your filing is to make any last minute property transfers or purchases!

Making last minute transactions is a major red flag in the bankruptcy process! It is imperative that you conduct any kind of property transfers or purchases at least SIX MONTHS in advance of your filing!

I have heard of people filing for bankruptcy that have actually taken out cash advances and set the money aside knowing that after they filed their bankruptcy they would be facing new problems.

After filing bankruptcy it can be difficult renting a place to live with anyone who runs your credit prior to renting.

For that reason I can remember hearing of one couple who set aside almost $20,000 in cash they held in their private safe so that they would be able to deal with problems such as home or apartment rental and other things.

One thing that can be difficult for people who file bankruptcy and are used to living with credit is the loss of that credit.

The world after filing for bankruptcy becomes a cash and/or debit card world.

AGAIN, A GOOD POLICY FOR ANY KIND OF TRANSACTION IS THAT IT BE COMPLETED AT LEAST **SIX MONTHS** PRIOR TO FILING!

As you will learn from your attorney consultations, if you are filing a Chapter 7 bankruptcy you should not claim to have more than about $50.00 cash on hand.

Another very important item involves your bank accounts. It is imperative that you close any bank accounts (both savings and checking) with any banks where you have accounts that you will be including in your bankruptcy!

If you have a Visa or MasterCard with your local bank and you are including those accounts in your bankruptcy then you need to close those bank accounts!

One other very important thing to realize is that even if you are reaffirming a debt held by your local bank and are also filing bankruptcy on credit card accounts or other unsecured loans carried by that same bank … YOU NEED TO CLOSE THAT SAVINGS OR CHECKING ACCOUNT(S) WITH YOUR BANK(S)!

I can assure you that the best policy is to close any open savings or checking accounts prior to filing your bankruptcy.

This especially applies where you have any loans or charge accounts or your pay check or any other deposits automatically made into those accounts.

The best policy is to close all of those accounts prior to filing.

It is crucial that you open new checking and savings accounts with banks you know are not related to any of your debt you are filing on!

WHY YOU MAY ASK?

Just think about what it would be like if you were to find out that none of your funds were available from your automatic pay check deposit.

Just think if the bank placed a freeze on all of your funds and your bank account and you had just sent out checks to pay all of your utility bills and your rent or mortgage payment?

Aside from all of the check bounce charges and fees what would happen to all of those accounts you made payments on with bad checks?

What would happen when all of a sudden you did not have access to money you had counted on from your paycheck funds?

Now you have no money available from your paycheck to live on … nothing available to you to pay your bills with … not even the money you need to make your home mortgage payment!

You will be very upset with yourself for not taking care of this ahead of time by opening new bank accounts where you clearly had no past indebtedness!

Thinking About Opening a New Bank Account?

A lot of smaller banks and credit unions cannot afford the fees associated with having their own Visa and MasterCard Services so they turn to larger banks to handle their Visa and MasterCard Accounts.

These smaller banks and credit unions contract with the larger banks to handle there credit card accounts.

If you file on a Visa or MasterCard Account that you did not get through your home bank directly but one of these accounts is actually carried by your home bank then you are essentially filing on your home bank!

This is why it is always a safe bet to just open new accounts with a new bank where you know you and your funds are safe.

PLAY IT SAFE! If you have money in any account with a bank that you feel is in any way associated with your home bank then close that account!

The associated bank may try to place a freeze on your account or just take your funds to recover the home banks losses!

This may be entirely illegal but you may still not be able to stop them at all! Why take chances with your money!

Just close any questionable bank accounts and go with a new bank and a new debit card and all.

Acquiring New Credit Cards

I have heard of couples who got new credit cards and only used them as cash cards paying off all balances by the end of each month.

They knew that the bankruptcy rules required persons to list all of their creditors so made certain that these new cards were paid to $0.00 prior to filing.

Since each of their new credit cards had a $0.00 balance they knew it would not be necessary to list them on their bankruptcy petition.

Of course when acquiring new credit cards you need to, once again, be certain that they are not related to any of the creditors or banks listed on the bankruptcy petition.

So in essence you need to be certain which bank is carrying any new credit card accounts you are thinking of adding. You need to make sure they are not affiliates of any creditors you are filing bankruptcy against.

Student Loans

I have heard of many cases where people filing chapter 7 bankruptcy had large Student Loans they also wanted to be paid off through the bankruptcy process.

Of course in almost all cases school loans are priority and would not be liquidated through bankruptcy.

What many of these people evidently did was to take cash advances on their credit cards that could be listed on their bankruptcy and paid off all of their School Loans with those cash advances!

They did this in unobvious ways by maybe taking smaller cash advances over a period of time and at least (6) or more months in advance of filing their bankruptcy

AGAIN A GOOD POLICY IS THAT THIS ACTION BE COMPLETED **NO LESS THAN SIX TO EIGHT MONTHS PRIOR** TO FILING!

I have heard numerous times of couples going to places like Las Vegas to get their cash advances so they would appear to have a bad gambling habit. In this way it was the gambling habit that became the focus rather than the cash advances.

By going to places like Las Vegas the real issue became a bad gambling habit rather than what they were actually doing with their cash advance money. The Little Stinkers!

Everything you do in the bankruptcy process is subject to question so following the corporate or bank model is the best practice at all times. What that means is "the less paper trail/documentation the better" which is the corporate motto as well.

Let the Banking & Credit Industry be your Role Model!

Just look at the 13 trillion dollar bank bail out where no one knows anything about where any of our tax dollar money disappeared to!   All of those millions just seemed to vanish into thin air!

http://www.pbs.org/wgbh/pages/frontline/shows/credit/view/

Just behave like the banks you are filing bankruptcy on.

Now it is your turn to treat the Banks and Credit Industry just as they have treated you.

Of course you are no match for these crooks who have absconded with billions of our tax dollars using our bail out money to pay out millions of dollars in annual bonuses they gave to themselves as bank executives and worse!

Of course you cannot be nearly as heinous as the banks and creditor corporations who have shafted us all but you can do everything possible to take care of yourself and your family.

They have absconded with all of our money and of course this travesty of a new bankruptcy law they paid so many millions to bribe our congress to set into law!

Just conduct your business along the same guidelines as the banking industry and the corporate world and you will do just fine!

If you plan on filing your bankruptcy in the next few months there are several things you can plan out ahead of time.

For instance, I have heard of persons who were planning to file for their bankruptcy selling off personal property to help create a post bankruptcy survival fund and so they made certain to take care of these transactions at least (6) months prior to filing bankruptcy.

Some have even taken cash advances to assure their survival!

These people made certain to sell off major belongings like motor homes ... boats vehicles ... gun collections ... coin collections ... and whatever else they wanted to liquidate for cash at least (6) months prior to filing their bankruptcy.

They knew that the trustee could not go back more than 180 days to collect those monies.

AGAIN ... A GOOD POLICY WITH ANY OF THESE ACTIONS IS THAT THEY ARE COMPLETED **AT LEAST SIX MONTHS PRIOR TO FILING YOUR BANKRUPTCY!**

There are many who also wanted to pay off certain creditor(s) because they wanted to keep their credit accounts in good standing and knew to do that at least (6) months prior to filing.

For instance, people who liked their medical doctor or dentist or other local professional made certain to pay them off so they would not be required to list them on their bankruptcy petition.

Please understand that friends and family you owe money to are also creditors just like any other creditors you are filing bankruptcy on. You must list all creditors.

The bankruptcy court requires that you list <u>all</u> creditors on your bankruptcy petition ... This is not an option!

You can decide to pay off family and personal friend creditors after completion of your bankruptcy.

What you do after you file your bankruptcy is entirely up to you.

If you do decide to pay any of these creditors it is best to just wait until you have received final notice from the bankruptcy court that your debt has all been discharged.

Watch the Timing! (More Insider Tricks of the Trade)

One of the key decisions you make affecting every aspect of your bankruptcy including which chapter you can file is **WHEN** you file your bankruptcy.

The question of WHEN really needs to be a decision you make yourself rather than having your situation decide for you.

If you are on the run and are in a panic because you are being pursued by your creditors and are continually harassed by them … Then your CREDITORS are
IN CONTROL … and that scenario will serve you little.

The last thing you want when you are filing bankruptcy is to file because you are feeling desperate and on the run from bill collectors.

You want to file when it is the absolute best time for you so that you will get exactly what you know is the best solution possible for your particular situation.

Above all you want to get the outcome that you desire and not what the banks and creditors desire of you!

For instance, if you run to an attorney because you are feeling desperate and are just plain tired of all the hassling from bill collectors … and you file your bankruptcy immediately to stop the harassment … and your income is too high … then **you can be forced into filing a Chapter 13 bankruptcy** which can go on for the next (5) years!

If on the contrary you plan out your bankruptcy well ahead of time and choose your absolute best time to file you can be saving yourself a huge amount of grief and money.

If you let your plan determine the best time for you to file instead of the creditors who are harassing you then you have taken control of the situation and will be able reap the benefits of filing Chapter 7 Bankruptcy!

In this case you will thank yourself repeatedly in the months or even years to come.

Remember, it is never a good idea to make any decision when you are uncertain or feeling pressured by outside forces.

Move at your own pace in harmony with your spirit and you cannot go wrong.

You May Ask "Why Watch the Timing?"

Well let's take the situation where you are on the run and you just want to end the creditor and bill collector hell you may have found yourself living in.

Let's say that the attorney looks at your income and you take the "MEANS Test" and the result tells you that you must file Chapter13 Bankruptcy.

Let's say that because of your income at that time you ran into the attorney's office required you to file chapter 13 bankruptcy with a payment that comes out to $450 per month.

Let's go further and say that your plan has been set for a (5) year payment period.

That means you will be paying your creditors $27,000.00 over the next (5) year period!

Let's say instead that because you already purchased this publication from me that you knew you only wanted to file for Chapter 7 Bankruptcy because you did your evaluation and realized that you had nothing to gain by filing Chapter 13 bankruptcy.

IN THIS SCENARIO YOU JUST SAVED YOURSELF A NICE $27,000.00!

So just out of curiosity how many years would it take you to save $27,000.00 if you begin setting extra money aside from your current income beginning today?

The benefits here are cumulative.   Now you will be able to restore your credit in as soon as six months after your bankruptcy filing!

If you had to file Chapter 13 Bankruptcy, the time required for you to have New Credit would be (5) years plus six months or 5 ½ years!

You can avoid all of this wasted time and have your New Credit back in as little as SIX MONTHS because you have purchased "Ultimate Credit

2010" or 'How to Have Your Good Credit Back Just Six Months After Bankruptcy'.

So now after just (6) months or so you have great credit and can even begin to focus on purchasing a replacement home for the one you may have surrendered or lost through foreclosure or the bankruptcy filing process itself!

Does it pay to Pre-Plan and Plan out your Bankruptcy … YOU BET IT DOES!

If you have taken CONTROL of your situation by choosing your time to file and by having a workable solution for dealing with all of those creditors then the rewards can be immense for you and your family.

How Can I Postpone Bankruptcy When Being Harassed?

You may be wondering "but how can I deal with all of my creditors who are driving me crazy ... calling at all times of the day and night ... some very rude ... many very hostile and demanding?

How can I deal with all of these evil people now before they drive me crazy?

One way you can put off filing your bankruptcy and at the same time get all of the vicious creditors and collection agencies off of your back is to enroll in a Consumer Credit Counseling Program!

This will assure that your bankruptcy plan will not be sabotaged and at the same time make you really look good to the bankruptcy court!

Simply enroll in a Consumer Credit Counseling Program and make payments through their program until you reach the ideal time for bankruptcy relief!

By enrolling with a Consumer Credit Counseling Service you will be getting the creditors temporarily off of your back and stopping the harassment!

If you go to the end of this publication you will see resources linked right from the U.S. Bankruptcy Court!

There you will find "Consumer Credit Counseling Services" who will set you up with an affordable payment plan that you will use temporarily until you actually file bankruptcy.

Help Is On the Way (U.S. Bankruptcy Court)

http://www.usdoj.gov/ust/eo/bapcpa/ccde/index.htm

http://www.usdoj.gov/ust/eo/bapcpa/ccde/docs/FTC_Consumer_AlertCC.pdf

Remember that you have your Plan to follow and that CCCS is merely a temporary fix until you file Bankruptcy.

Make sure that when you go into Consumer Credit Counseling Services to sign up that you do not let them know you are a temporary client!

The only value Consumer Credit Counseling Service will have for you is to get the creditors off of your back until you are ready to file your bankruptcy!

The other benefit of using Consumer Credit Counseling Services is that they are creditor oriented and so you look good to the bankruptcy court.

The reason that you will be looking so good is that you have attempted to deal with your debt problems in a responsible manner with an organization that the creditor industry supports.

In reality most people feel that these Consumer Credit Counseling Services are way too creditor oriented and leave the client with little or nothing for each month to live on ... so once again ... you need to take control here!

You don't have to be totally up front with these guys because they are not a branch of the government and have no real authority.

Once again when dealing with Consumer Credit Counseling Services you need to TAKE CONTROL BY NEGOTIATING YOUR PAYMENT PLAN!

When you are doing your income to debt ratio work ... you need to be the one who sets your expenses at a level that you can afford to live with!

If both spouses are working, it might be easier to lower your estimates in this area by one of you quitting their job or not reporting the income if it is under the table.

Remember you will no doubt be asked to bring in pay check stubs soooo ... be aware of what you are doing here.

Also, the counselors you will meet with will know if you are inflating your expenses so be cautious ... don't over do it!

You need to be able to prove your claims with receipts if necessary.

Just know that CCCS Counselors can be brutal with cost of living issues!

I have had people come in for their bankruptcy consultation that were given only $50 per month to live on after their plan payment was made and the consumer credit counseling fee was paid … I am not making this up!

That $50 per month that was left for them was supposed to cover groceries, utilities, medical, gasoline and all of their general living expenses!   Did someone say Duh?

The credit counselor that did their budget and payment plan did not seem to care much about what they were planning for my clients!

All they really seemed to care about was servicing the creditors and collecting the consumer credit counselor fees!

The fact is that these credit counselors work for the Credit Industry and they can be just as greedy as those creditors they are working for!

Too often the credit counselors want way too much for the creditors so remember to be prepared once again to negotiate.

If you question the greediness factor of the Credit Industry, just look at the state of our economy today, just look at where so much of the American People's Wealth has gone to?

Anyway, this is a completely different topic from what we are dealing with here … well kinda …

Another alternative you have is to just avoid or ignore your creditors completely but this can be risky and embarrassing decision!

Many people change their telephone numbers and relocate … and do whatever they need to in order to avoid any contact with their creditors.

Just remember that Creditors can take you to court and then come after your wages!

Some creditors will call your neighbors and start asking all kinds of very embarrassing questions like "does so and so usually pay their bills on time?" or "Is so and so usually considered a reliable and responsible person?" and other forms of harassment behavior many of which are totally illegal!

Also, the last thing that you want for a number of reasons is a Wage Garnishment.

If you value employment with your current employer and the ability to pay your bills and cost of living expenses then a wage garnishment is not the way to go.

Some employers frown on Wage Garnishments and so it a good thing to avoid.

When is the best time to make my move?

The answer to this question is … RIGHT NOW!

If you have purchased this publication, you have more than likely already decided that you will be filing bankruptcy at some time in the near future.

If this is the case, then NOW is the time to make your move and to begin by scheduling your Free Bankruptcy Consultations.

This will truly be the beginning of your bankruptcy education and gathering of crucial information you will need to get the fresh start your filing bankruptcy can give you.

What you will learn over the next few weeks with your Bankruptcy Consultations is which chapter of bankruptcy will best serve your future needs and plans.

You will learn which bankruptcy chapter will allow you to put Your Plan into action and move you on the path that you have pre-defined for your ideal outcome!

In time you will learn the one key element of your bankruptcy petition that will determine many things including what chapter of the bankruptcy code you can file under.

That one key element is … **YOUR BUDGET**.

If Your Plan Calls For Chapter 7 Bankruptcy

In a previous example I described a situation that ended up unnecessarily costing the consumer $27,000.00! This happened because they were unprepared and their income to debt ratio defined in the "means test" required them to file Chapter 13 Bankruptcy instead of chapter 7.

In the example a Chapter 7 Bankruptcy was far more preferable for that consumer.
The problem is that the person filing had not planned out their strategy in advance and ended up being a victim of a process that they really could have benefited from.

If they would have planned their bankruptcy out in advance they would have saved $27,000.00 in unnecessary expense!

If the difference between your income and your expenditures is too great and you have excess $$$ available to you each month and will not be able to file under Chapter 7 of the Bankruptcy Code!

It is your income to debt ratio listed on Schedules I & J that determines the result you will obtain in your "means test".

If you wish to resolve an excess income issue because your plan is to file Chapter 7 Bankruptcy then you have basically two choices:

ONE OF TWO THINGS MUST HAPPEN TO ADDRESS THIS PROBLEM:

1. Your income must decrease because of less hours or change in employment or your spouse becomes unemployed, etc.

http://www.uscourts.gov/rules/BK_Forms_1207/B_006I_1207f.pdf

- OR -

2. Your expenditures increase your cost of living by an amount that will zero out any positive net difference between income and debt claimed.

http://www.uscourts.gov/rules/BK_Forms_1207/B_006J_1207f.pdf

If your expenses increase they must do so by an amount that is very Realistic and Explainable so it will be acceptable to the Bankruptcy Trustee!

Your Bankruptcy Attorney will be your best resource for help with this matter because they will know the numbers that the trustee generally Is ok with and will avoid any red flags.

So you need to be aware that the actual timing when you file your bankruptcy can be crucial!

Choosing the right time can be a very important strategic decision that can determine everything related to your bankruptcy.

In these times of a heavily unstable job market and economy, it can be difficult to determine or predict just what might be coming next.

The current unemployment situation in this country can actually help you take control of your bankruptcy and choose the Bankruptcy Chapter you can file under.

The severity of the economic crisis that exists in our country right now will make it far easier to validate what ever actions you may need to take in order to resolve the income to debt issue.   I guess this is one thing we can thank the Banks for!

So the point here is that you file your bankruptcy when things in your life situation make your filing the most beneficial to you and your family.

Many persons filing for Chapter 7 Bankruptcy have decided to make plans that include taking some time off from work and collecting unemployment for a three or four month period as needed. This can give you a badly needed vacation and save you a minimum of $20,000 Plus a whole lot of grief!

Remember that the dollar amount saved is not your number one consideration when filing for bankruptcy.

You need to figure in all factors when identifying what works best for you.

You need to consider everything including assets you need to protect, IRS debt you need to resolve, a home that is in arrearage or is heading into foreclosure, plus a lot of other considerations that will affect your life after bankruptcy.

Once again the best way to determine your bankruptcy strategy is with the help of your Bankruptcy Attorney who can spell out the options that will best serve your particular needs.

Since you are planning your future here it is very important for you to know in advance what kind of outcome you can expect.

You POWER in this process is founded in the KNOWLEDGE you have gained as a result of my Bankruptcy Control System and by your putting that knowledge to work for you.

Right Now is the best time to make the decision on what Chapter of the Bankruptcy Code you will eventually want to file under!

If Chapter 7 Bankruptcy works best for you then you may need to wait for a gap period in your employment situation and file at the beginning of that gap.

It may also be imperative that you have money set aside or have credit cards that you can use to purchase your food and cover your other necessary costs of living.

If you can file unemployment during this gap then all the better!

The next thing you need to look at is how to create a realistic budget without creating any RED FLAGS.

Just how much should you claim on your living expense side of the budget?

When you are creating your budget remember one thing above all; this is the budget you will be expected to live on either during (if Ch. 13) or after your bankruptcy is filed!

What do I mean here? If you claim $200 per month for groceries then guess what? If you file under Chapter 13 of the Bankruptcy Code then $200 is what you will be forced to live on to cover all of your grocery expenses!

When you think about budget you need to take into account EVERYTHING you are spending on a daily … weekly … and on a monthly basis.

You need to look at what you buy when you shop at Walmart for instance? You need to know what real world purchases you regularly make and account for every one of them in your budget?

You need to create this real world budget in such a manner as to not provoke and cause the wrath of the bankruptcy trustee!

The real question is, "How do you create a real world budget that the bankruptcy trustee will feel is reasonable and not offensive in any way?"

One good way to avoid red flags and hassles in the bankruptcy court is to be both realistic with your numbers and above all BE SPECIFIC!

What do I mean by SPECIFIC? Break everything down into categories.

When you go to Target, Walmart, Trader Joes or Costco break down how you spend your money into specific categories.

GROCERY/FOOD: (Make sure you get everything) (i.e. $300 per mo.)

Produce

Meats
Mixes
Beverages
etc

Household Goods: (i.e. $75 per mo.)
Cleanser
Bleach
dishwashing liquid
sponges
furniture polish
shoe polish
paper towels
toilet paper
pet food
etc

MEDICAL: (Make sure you cover everything!)

Doctor visits
Medications
Dental visits
Co-pay Doctor
Co-pay Dental
Co-pay Medications
Vitamin Supplements
Chiropractic
Gym

INSURANCE: (Specify all insurance)

Home owners Insurance
Home Repair Insurance
Health/Medical Insurance
Car Insurance
Life Insurance

Some of the above items might be considered questionable to the U.S.
Bankruptcy Court. So work with your attorney on where to list them and

make sure that all of these areas are accounted for. Make sure not to over inflate your claimed $$$ amounts or they will create a definite RED FLAG and that means trouble!

One thing I will say when pre-planning your bankruptcy is to **NEVER ASSUME**!

If there is any single area or item where you are not certain then **ASK YOUR ATTORNEY!** This is why you are paying your legal representation so use this resource to help you make everything work for you.

Your attorney will be very familiar with how the trustee handles claimed costs of living and should be able to direct you when you try to go beyond what the trustee usually approves.

Make certain that your numbers are not set too low as well just to make the attorney's job easier or make him look good in the trustee's eyes.

Your bankruptcy is about you and not your Bankruptcy Attorney or the Trustee.

Just make sure that your cost of living is covered realistically. In other words be ready to negotiate everything with your attorney. Do not just say yes to everything because it seems the easiest thing to do at the time.

You may regret having been so cooperative with your attorney a few weeks down the road when you actually have to live according to those claimed expenses.

Better to get your work done up front and then you can rest once you are pleased with the result.

I have commented that filing for bankruptcy is like applying for a part time job because the end result of your efforts is directly related to your spendable income and especially where Chapter 13 bankruptcy is concerned.

You will be rewarded several times over for very little effort you put out in your pre-planning!

If you are filing chapter 13 bankruptcy and your monthly plan payment would have been $800 per month prior to using my "Bankruptcy Control System" and the result of doing your work here has reduced your payment to $100 per month … you are getting back a huge benefit for your purchase of this publication.

Considering that your Chapter 13 Bankruptcy Plans are usually set to run for a (5) year period we are talking about a great deal of $$$ savings here!

In fact, in the above scenario you have gone from $9,600 per year to $1,200 per year and this is a saving of $8,400 per year!

If You Are in a Chapter 13 Bankruptcy Plan then You Just SAVED Yourself a Nice $42,000 over the (5) year period of the plan!

THAT IS A $42,000 SAVINGS over five years and is the equivalent of giving yourself a $700 per month pay raise (or there about) in this example!

THIS IS THE STIMULUS PACKAGE THAT NO ONE EVER GAVE YOU BUT YOU HAVE CREATED FOR YOURSELF!

The most important thing is that you do your work now and reap the benefits for years to come and truly create a NEW LIFE for yourself free of debt and free of the misery that accompanies your current indebtedness scenario!

If as a result of doing your work, as described in this publication, you have been able to file a Chapter 7 Bankruptcy then you have learned well. I say this because you realize that there are no real benefits to you by filing chapter 13.

In this case you have saved even more money and are truly saving yourself much pain and suffering by not having to file Chapter 13.

What I am saying is that if you do your budget work correctly and make certain you watch the timing when you file and only file when it is in your best interest (the timing can be critical) that by doing so you can save yourself much grief and money as well.

You can save yourself the kind of long term commitment that is required when filing a Chapter 13 Bankruptcy and especially when it is of no real benefit to you.

You can lower your Chapter 13 Bankruptcy payments when the amount you are paying is simply not necessary to help you resolve your financial issues like mortgage arrearages or IRS Debt.

If filing a Chapter 13 Bankruptcy serves no real purpose for you, then you need to ask yourself what you are doing filing under the Chapter 13 Bankruptcy Code?

In fact the consensus among people filing bankruptcy is that if you are not protecting key assets like your home(s) or not paying off school loan(s) or IRS debt or any issue that requires your filing chapter 13 then you need to work hard to qualify under the chapter 7 bankruptcy code!

You need to qualify for a Chapter 7 Bankruptcy and do this with the help of the Bankruptcy Attorney you have retained. If you feel your attorney is holding back or not willing to really get involved with helping you … get another attorney!

The changes in the bankruptcy law that the member of congress working for MBNA pushed through … when he was still in congress … and was supposedly working for the American people (and not the credit industry) … pretty much re-focused the bankruptcy court away from helping the consumer … to servicing the creditor and banking industry.

That same member of congress retired from his "Serving the People" position in congress weeks after he got the new bankruptcy law passed and weeks later was made the C.E.O. of MBNA!

(MBNA was not going to make this congressman head of MBNA for nothing!) (He had to act as traitor to the American People first so that MBNA could pay him off for his loyal servitude! (MBNA is now owned by

Bank of America - through Mergers & Acquisitions)   Hmmmmm … such a very small world … isn't it?)

Paragraph below from Wikipedia with my added comments in parenthesis:

MBNA was one of the prime movers in lobbying for the passage of the Bankruptcy Abuse Prevention and Consumer Protection Act of 2005, which took 11 years and **millions of dollars spent on lobbying before the act was finally passed** when 15 Democrats (all of whom had received campaign contributions from MBNA, notably Joseph R. Biden, Jr. (D-DE) $147,700) joined with their Republican colleagues to sign it into law.[citation needed]

ALSO: http://www.pbs.org/wgbh/pages/frontline/shows/credit/view/

What you need to do now is compensate for everything you can that the MBNA owned puppet congressman did to you and generations to come with this new bend over and take it in your bankruptcy act.

What Chapter of Bankruptcy you will end up filing will be largely determined by you through your "means test" and your income to debt ratio. If you have followed the guidelines here your plan will ultimately be determined by my Bankruptcy Control System Plan!

So the chapter you will ultimately file will be based upon your particular need based upon my Bankruptcy Control System Plan.

Ultimately the chapter you file needs to be completely determined by you and not your attorney or anyone else!

This is something you will learn by asking all of the right questions during your Free Bankruptcy Consultations.

This topic is also the one that you will need to discuss with your attorney to determine which chapter is right for your particular need.

No Matter What Chapter you end up filing under the above Information Applies.

So what is the problem described in a previous example I used that ended up costing you $27,000 in a chapter 13 that could have been avoided?

The problem was clearly that Chapter 13 was chosen when it offered no real advantage at all to the party filing bankruptcy. In that case the party would have been far better off filing Chapter 7 Bankruptcy instead,

On the flip side of that, If your plan was to pay arrearages on your mortgage and the amount you are delinquent comes out to say $25,000 then this budget is close to what you will need.

The budget for a chapter 13 plan paid out over 5 years must reflect the amount of the arrearage.

So you would start by dividing 5 yrs into 260 weeks. Take the arrearage amount of $25,000 and divide by 260 weeks = $160.25 X 52 for one year = $4,999.80 per year divided by 12 months = approximate monthly of $416.65 per month.

If the difference between your income and expenditures is around $417 per month, give or take a few $$$, then your plan payment will be $417 per month. (You need to remember that your plan payment needs to include 3% for the court fee in order for your chapter 13 bankruptcy to be workable!)

If there are more items that need to be added into your Chapter 13 Bankruptcy Plan you will need to make the proper adjustments in your income to debt ratio.

For instance, if you have IRS debt or school loan debt or child support debt then this must also be figured in and your plan payment adjusted to reflect the change.

Your income to debt ratio will also need to provide the extra money for your plan to cover the addition of any new plan payment items as well.

Discuss this matter with your Bankruptcy Attorney even if you are not in doubt and have them explain how it all needs to be figured in.

It is your income to debt ratio shown on your schedules I & J plus your "means test" that will determine what Bankruptcy Chapter will work for you.

If you have income to debt issues to resolve because your plan is to file Chapter 13 Bankruptcy and Schedules I & J are not in agreement with your Bankruptcy Control Plan then you have basically two choices:

IT IS CRITICALLY IMPORTANT THAT YOU UNDERSTAND THIS AREA OF THE BANKRUPTCY FILING PROCESS!

    1. Your income must increase or decrease.

    http://www.uscourts.gov/rules/BK_Forms_1207/B_006I_1207f.pdf

    - OR -

    2. Your expenditures must increase or decrease.

    http://www.uscourts.gov/rules/BK_Forms_1207/B_006J_1207f.pdf

When properly adjusted your Income to Debt Ratio for a Chapter 13 Bankruptcy (schedules I & J) would allow for the plan payment amount you seek plus about 2% left over for the unsecured creditors.

This means that you have taken into account all mandatory pay-offs of your chapter 13 Plan which would include all Priority and Secured Debt for secured property that you wish to re-affirm and keep.

In other words the difference between Schedule I & J would be equal to a positive amount left over that covers all mandatory and priority debt you must pay off in your plan plus about 2% added to be paid to your unsecured creditors. ("unsecured creditors" would include things like credit card debt, medical bills, collection accounts and the like)

If your plan calls for you to file Chapter 13 and you do not have the verifiable income to cover the cost of your plan payment plus your cost of living expenses then the Bankruptcy Court can deny your filing under that chapter.

In that case your spouse may need to take a job if they are not working at the time to make your Chapter 13 Bankruptcy Plan workable.

If your plan calls for you to file Chapter 7 Bankruptcy then your expenses must Increase by an amount that is very realistic and explainable to the bankruptcy trustee for a chapter 7 bankruptcy … and/or

Your income must Decrease by an amount that is in line with the amount required for your Chapter 7 to work!

Sometimes this may require the spouse to quit their job if they are already working because the income figure is pretty much a fixed item that cannot be changed that easily without a change in employment.

If you see unemployment on the horizon then you know that you need to wait to file your Chapter 7 Bankruptcy and not file now while you are gainfully employed because this could throw you into a Chapter 13 Bankruptcy and a headache and added expenses that you do not need!

Your Bankruptcy Attorney will be your best resource for help with this matter since they know the numbers that the trustee generally is ok with and will know how to avoid any Red Flags.

So you need to be aware of and design the actual timing that is best for you to file your bankruptcy and that can be crucial!

Choosing the right time can be a very important strategic decision that will determine everything related to your bankruptcy.

In these times of a heavily unstable job market and economy it can be difficult to determine or predict just what might be coming next so use this factor to your advantage.

What Happens To Unsecured Debt In Chapter 13 Bankruptcy?

The Chapter 13 Bankruptcy is set up in a way that allows you to pay arrearages with any secured debt through affordable monthly payments commonly over a plan that is (5) years in length.

This plan may contain mortgage payment arrearages, income tax debt, school loan debt, etc plus a percentage of your unsecured debt.

In a Chapter 13 Bankruptcy your unsecured creditors get what is left after all of your priority debts are paid.

If we use the example from before where your arrearages on your mortgage total $25,000 and are all that you have to deal with in your Chapter 13 Plan then your Plan Payments are going to be about $416.65 per month.   lets look at what might happen to your unsecured debt in this situation.

Lets take a scenario where you have just the arrearages on your home and $50,000 in unsecured debt and after completing your income to debt ratio (income and expenditure statements) you have just $525 left over per month.

Your disbursement of money might look something like $416 per month toward the mortgage arrearages plus 3% to the bankruptcy court for service fees and the rest or approximately $93 per month divided up among all of the unsecured creditors.

What this means is that in a (5) year plan the unsecured creditors will get a total of $5,580 by the end of the five year period!

What happens to the other $44,420 of unsecured debt? That total amount of debt is discharged as best effort loss!

This is referred to is "Best Effort" because it is based on the fact that the debtor has made every effort to pay off their creditors in their plan payment and as much of the unsecured non priority debt that they could afford at the time.

This scenario also accounts for the debtor having to live and so takes into account a reasonable cost of living for the (5) year period.

At the end of the (5) year period what happens most of the time is that all of the unsecured debt simply goes away.

Discuss this matter with your Bankruptcy Attorney to be certain that your plan has been effectively laid out with all factors taken into account.

Things to Avoid No Matter What

There are a few things that you may be tempted to do as a part of your bankruptcy filing that you need to avoid at all costs:

Over Inflated or Under Estimated Budget

When preparing your budget do not over or under estimate your budget figures!

This is especially true when you are qualifying for filing Chapter 7 Bankruptcy.

Discuss the figures you have chosen with your Bankruptcy Attorney because they will know through experience with the Chapter 13 Court just what the trustee will find acceptable or what may cause a Red Flag.

Also remember that for a Chapter 13 Bankruptcy it is not wise to under estimate your cost of living expenses because these are the numbers you will be forced to live with during the full (3) to (5) year period of your Chapter 13 Bankruptcy.

Remember that you will be forced to live with these figures more likely than not for a period of from (3) to (5) years!

By the same token do not over estimate your living costs as a means to lower your chapter 13 plan payment amount!

If you set your expenses too high according to what is allowable by the bankruptcy trustee then your claims will be objected to and you can be forced to refigure your numbers.

If your cost of living figures are too inflated in your schedule J which is your expenditures statement and you are filing for Chapter 7 Bankruptcy then the trustee could possibly even force you into filing Chapter 13 Bankruptcy!

Schedule J – Current Expenditures

http://www.uscourts.gov/rules/BK_Forms_1207/B_006J_1207f.pdf

need to discuss with your attorney what the trustee will generally allow for cost of living expenses for the chapter you are filing.

Your attorney will know because he sees what is approved and rejected on a regular basis with the bankruptcy trustee and judge in your district.

Withholding Sources of Income

Make certain that you report all sources of income even if you feel a source cannot be traced.

You could have a hidden source of income and not report it to the bankruptcy court.

Then one day you have a dispute with the source providing your hidden income and if they know about your bankruptcy they could decide to report you for withholding income information.

They could report this information to the bankruptcy court because maybe they are really angry with you and want to get even for any real or imagined wrong doing by you.

That could be grounds to dismiss your bankruptcy or to even nail you for fraud!

Remember you are dealing with the federal government so be watchful and cautious with any decision related to your finances and ultimately your bankruptcy.

Not reporting key assets

The bankruptcy is offering you pretty much total relief from your indebtedness and a truly fresh start if you handle your bankruptcy responsibly.

In exchange for this assistance by the bankruptcy court you are agreeing to report all sources of income and all assets you own or have liquidated in recent history.

As with most things in life the best policy here is honesty!

Debts That May Not Be Discharged (could mean worse!)

- Debts resulting from Fraudulent behavior
- False written statement to creditor regarding your financial condition
- Cash Advances in excess of $800.00 within (90) days of filing for bankruptcy
- Debts for luxury items that were charged within (6) months of your filing
- Creditors or Debts you fail to list on your bankruptcy petition
- taking cash advances to pay off priority debt such as school loans or child support within (6) months of filing bankruptcy and when the monies were clearly used to pay off this kind of non-dischargeable debt
- Debts related to commitment of Larceny, Embezzlement or breach of fiduciary duty
- Debts resulting from willful or malicious acts

CREDIT CARD FRAUD - Possible Objections from Creditors:

- Spending Sprees within (6) months of filing for bankruptcy
- Telling creditor they are filing for bankruptcy prior to running up additional charges

- Run ups or spending sprees that occurred after the date on Attorney Fee Statement
- Charges made after debtor was already delinquent on payments or was clearly unable to pay back the debt
- Charges made after creditor has requested you destroy your card or return it
- Repeated charges under $50 when debtor has hit their credit limit (doing this in order to get approval due to small amount of each charge)
- Rapid increase in spending followed by little use at all
- A short time between repeated charging right before filing for bankruptcy
- Charges made when debtor was clearly in financial trouble and had no intention of paying it back

NOTE: In all of these cases I purposely use conservative time frames for any of your charging activities and for good reason!

The last thing you want in your bankruptcy petition is Red Flag appearing for any reason!

From what I have heard a SIX MONTH PERIOD for any activity is best if it could be construed as fraudulent or questionable by either the bankruptcy trustee or the creditors!

Sale of Property

If you have non-exempt personal property you wish to liquidate prior to your filing for bankruptcy please do not try selling your car to your cousin for $1.00!

If you try something lame like this you are asking for trouble plain and simple!

When one RED FLAG shows up in your paperwork it may produce greater scrutiny over every element in your paperwork and you do not want this happening with your petition!

You do not want unnecessary hassles just because you are trying to claim some silly little item of little value to begin with. KEEP YOUR FOCUS ON THE OVER ALL PICTURE!

Keep your property values consistent and realistic at all times!

This rule of value applies also when looking at real world values of property you own. You may have things in your home that you value highly but that does not mean anything in the bankruptcy court!

For instance you may have a piece of jewelry that you value so highly and to you it is worth thousands of dollars.

A good guideline for evaluating property value is to ask yourself this question; "If you had to sell this item and had one week to do it, just how much do you think you would realistically get for it?"

Or if you have an older car that you think is really a collectible because it is years old and still in great shape you need to be honest with yourself.

"Is this really an antique automobile of great dollar value or simply a nice clean old automobile?"

Your vintage car may be worth a lot to you but if you had to sell it in one week just how much could you really get for it?

That is the method that the attorneys I have worked with have used to estimate property values and they were never challenged by the bankruptcy trustees.

Another factor to consider here is how much it would cost the trustee to take that property and actually sell it for its value?

There would be fees and costs just to liquidate the item and so its value would be further depreciated as well in that scenario.

Property Transfers and Purchases

As discussed above avoid making any property transfers or purchases prior to filing your bankruptcy because behavior like that shouts out attempted FRAUD!

You might have an extra car in the household that your son or daughter has been using for a couple of years and maybe has even paid for it but needed you to sign on the loan because of your credit was good at the time and theirs was not.

If you transferred that car to your son or daughter two months before filing for bankruptcy just ask yourself what that looks like to the bankruptcy court.

If your son or daughter can show a history of making all payments on this vehicle it will help your case for sure.
You are better off just explaining your situation to your attorney and letting your attorney tell you the best way to deal with this under the current climate of the bankruptcy court.

If you can hold to the guideline I mentioned before then make the title transfer at least SIX MONTHS prior to filing for bankruptcy.

If You Live In a "Community Property" State the Rules Change

If you are married and live in a community property state like I do in California then you need to be aware of how property ownership is determined!

If you and your spouse are separated for instance and you file for bankruptcy and your spouse does not file jointly it may not matter!

The court may still take both of your interests in any property you own.

In a community property state you both have shared ownership of all property.

Once again it is very important to discuss this issue with your Bankruptcy Attorney.

Tell All

It is imperative that you report all of your transactions as requested on your "Statement of Financial Affairs" and to leave nothing out.

You can explain that you did whatever was necessary to protect that personal property you valued most prior to filing. When you review this Statement, you will see that it goes back on average (90) days and in some cases one year.

http://www.uscourts.gov/rules/BK_Forms_1207/B_007_1207f.pdf

Peruse this form and discuss with your Bankruptcy Attorney if uncertain about what general information the court is seeking and how deal with this area.

Also review the instructions for this form as well to get a clearer picture of what the court is looking for.

http://www.uscourts.gov/rules/BK_Forms_1207/b7-inst.pdf

Other Things to Consider

Filing Declaration of Homestead in the state where you reside

There are only a few states that require you to file a formal Declaration of Homestead so make sure you discuss this with your Bankruptcy Attorney!

Avoid Having Any Debt Owed Directly to Bank(s)

(Overdraft or other fees/services)

YOU DO NOT WANT TO GET LISTED WITH "CHEXSYSTEMS"

http://en.wikipedia.org/wiki/ChexSystems

It is critical that you pay off any debt that you have with your bank(s) prior to filing for bankruptcy.

I am not talking about credit card debt like a Visa or MasterCard account with your bank.

You bank will list you with "ChexSystems" if you owe your bank money for services specifically provided to you by your bank.

This would pertain to money owed directly to your bank(s) for things like overdrafts or fraudulent checks.

If you have any bank fees or past due fees that are specifically with your bank(s) or any bank(s) then pay them all off before filing!

Most banks WILL NOT LET YOU OPEN ANOTHER BANK ACCOUNT OF ANY KIND ANYWHERE for a period of five years with any "CheckSystems" Member BANK!

LIFE IN AMERICA WITHOUT ANY KIND OF BANK ACCOUNT CAN BE A VERY DIFFICULT THING!

Creditors Holding Unsecured Priority Claims

Priority claims are those claims that are given priority in the bankruptcy court and pretty much exempts them from being liquidated as a part of your bankruptcy filing.

Examples of priority claims are School Loan Debt, IRS Debt, Child Support, Deposits by individuals (i.e. security deposit given to you for a rental), wages, salaries, commissions, and so on. See bankruptcy form below:

http://www.uscourts.gov/rules/BK_Forms_1207/B_006E_1207f.pdf

If you wish to challenge the priority status of any priority debt because you wish to have it discharged I believe you are really asking for trouble even if you have truly extenuating circumstances. I would not consider doing this and especially without the assistance of your Bankruptcy Attorney!

Once again discuss this matter with your Bankruptcy Attorney before making any final decision.

Saving your Home by filing chapter 13 bankruptcy

If you are behind in your mortgage payments then Chapter 13 can be your saving grace!

Chapter 13 Bankruptcy will allow you to pay out your total mortgage arrearage plus interest and penalty charges over a period of time according to what you can afford.

Say you are behind six months on your mortgage payments and are threatened with losing your home to foreclosure.

The Chapter 13 Bankruptcy will allow you to pay out your arrearage amount over a period of five years. Once you have filed your Chapter 13 Bankruptcy you will stop any new late fees and penalties from occurring.

If you are in the arrears on your first mortgage by six payments at a cost of $1,500 per month and current on your second mortgage then you will need to catch up by $9,000 plus any late fees and interest already charged.

The first thing you need to do is contact your mortgage company and get the total amount needed to bring your loan current.

Once you have this amount you will need to determine after reviewing your other plan payment debt just how much you will need for a (5) year Plan Payment.

If your arrearage is the only matter you need to spread out over time then you will need to take the $9,000 arrearage and convert into monthly payment that amount to $149.98 for 60 months to get caught up on that arrearage.

You would have to look at the total arrearage with fees included and figure in so much for the trustee fees but in the end probably $165 per month would cover it all!

When you are in a chapter 13 bankruptcy you must keep making all of your regularly scheduled mortgage payments plus your chapter 13 plan payment.

That is the deal! You pay all of your regularly scheduled mortgage payments and have enough left over for your plan payment and your cost of living expenses!

In order to qualify for this chapter 13 plan you must be able to afford your cost of living plus all of your secured payments plus your chapter 13 plan payment!

In this scenario once again your budget figures are critically important!

Dealing with IRS Debt by filing Chapter 7 Bankruptcy

If your IRS Debt has been owed for three or more years then it is eligible for discharge under Chapter 7 Bankruptcy. It is crucial that you discuss this matter with your Bankruptcy Attorney and learn all of the conditions required in order for this discharge to occur.

Dealing with IRS Debt by filing Chapter 13 Bankruptcy

If you have IRS Debt the chapter 13 bankruptcy can save you a lot of grief and money!

If you are being threatened with wage garnishments by the IRS and ideally if they have not started yet you can file for Chapter 13 Bankruptcy and you will effectively be stopping the wage garnishment.

You will not only be dealing with your wage garnishments but you will stop any further interest or penalty charges on your balance. (the amount owed will be locked-in once you start your Chapter 13 Bankruptcy.)

If you have been making IRS Plan Payments and feel that you are getting no where paying down your balance (because of continually added penalty and interest fees) you can file a Chapter 13 Bankruptcy and stop all penalties and late fees and pay off the debt with payments that you can afford.

As soon as you file your Chapter 13 Bankruptcy petition all interest and late fee/penalty charges are stopped!

If your situation is such, you can possibly file a Chapter 7 Bankruptcy and get all of your IRS debt discharged through your bankruptcy.   This is an item you really need to discuss with your Bankruptcy Attorney! If IRS debt is an issue for you then it would be best to discuss this matter with all of the Bankruptcy Attorney's you visit during your initial FREE BANKRUPTCY CONSULTATION phase of this process!

It may be possible that some of the Bankruptcy Attorneys you speak with may not know that IRS might be dischargeable so ask them all till you get an answer you are satisfied with.

You need to speak with your Bankruptcy Attorney regarding the rules and procedures required in order to have any IRS debt discharged through your Bankruptcy.

There may be certain conditions that must be complied with in order for this debt to qualify for discharge. Discuss with your Bankruptcy Attorney.

What Debt Can You Discharge Through Bankruptcy?

If no fraud or attempted fraud of any kind was committed then the majority of the following debts are usually dischargeable;

Credit card debt, debts from leases and contracts, debts from medical bills, debts from auto accidents, debts from lawsuits, debts from personal loans, debts from promissory notes, debts from judgments.

What Debt Can't Be Discharged Through Bankruptcy?

The following types of debt are not dischargeable under most if not any circumstances!

Child support, alimony, maintenance/support, debts owed to a spouse or child as a result of separation or divorce (does not apply to domestic partners), fines for violation of agency regulation, fines for infraction, restitution for federal criminal cases, bail bond debts related to bond forfeiture, misdemeanor or felony offenses, court levied surcharges for law enforcement, fines for time spent in a court jail, fines meant for punishment and levied by federal, state or local governments, election law fines or penalties, fraudulent income taxes (where no tax return has been filed (in fact you need to file all tax returns prior to filing your bankruptcy to assure you can get relief for past due income taxes), any debts resulting from killing or injuring someone while driving while intoxicated (either alcohol or drugs), payroll taxes, excise taxes, customs duties, sales & use tax.

More Dischargeable Debt

Debts you were unable to discharge in a previous bankruptcy filing, debts for retirement plan loans, condo, coop, homeowner assn fees, property taxes due for a year or more, income taxes three years or older where all tax returns have been filed with the IRS prior to filing your bankruptcy.

You can attempt to discharge your student loans if you think you have enough good reason but I would not count on it!

As always it is in your best interest to consult your attorney on all of these matters and anything not covered here!

ONCE AGAIN IT WOULD BE A GOOD POLICY TO ASK EVERY BANKRUPTCY ATTORNEY THAT YOU HAVE YOUR FREE BANKRUPTCY CONSULTATIONS WITH ABOUT SCHOOL LOAN DEBT!

It may be possible that some Bankruptcy Attorneys are not aware of the rules that apply to School Loans and if they can be discharged through bankruptcy.

State Exemptions

Double Exemptions: Married couples when filing jointly are permitted to double the exemption amounts with each claiming the full exemption when filing.

This practice varies from state to state so you will need to discuss all aspects of this issue with your Bankruptcy Attorney.

Remember that Exemptions Rules vary from state to state.

You can find the exemptions for the State and District where you reside and will be filing your bankruptcy at the end of this publication.

Check State Listing at End of This Publication under: **U.S. Bankruptcy Court Locations Nationwide**

Frequently Asked Questions

QUESTION: When filing Chapter 7 or Chapter 13 Bankruptcy is it a good idea to keep very much surplus money deposited in my bank account or anywhere that is traceable?

ANSWER: No matter what chapter of bankruptcy you are filing do you really think it is a wise idea in the current hostile bank & creditor climate to show additional money anywhere? In Chapter 7 bankruptcy you are saying you have to file because you are insolvent and thus have no money!

In a Chapter 13 you are saying you only have enough money to afford the plan payment you are making - so where is this extra money in your bank account(s) coming from?

If you are filing Chapter 13 and have a business then of course you will need to have operational funds in your accounts. In a Chapter 13 this is different from Chapter 7 where you can only have only minimum funds available to you.

Remember you may need to substantiate any funds you have that are in excess of those amounts you have claimed on Schedules I and J.

ALWAYS DISCUSS ANY QUESTIONS WITH YOUR BANKRUPTCY ATTORNEY.

There are some cases where I have heard that many people convert any excess monies into American Express Travelers Checks or Cashiers Checks but it is probably preferable to keep the extra funds in a fire proof safe that is heavily secured.

QUESTION: Is it a good idea to transfer title to one of my cars over to my son before i actually file for bankruptcy next month?

ANSWER: if you transfer your car or other personal property of any real value just one month or even two months before you file your bankruptcy then what do you think this behavior will look like to the bankruptcy trustee?

If you don't want to give the bankruptcy court an impression that you are trying to commit fraud by changing ownership or title to property just prior to your filing bankruptcy then i would avoid this kind of behavior.

I have a whole section in my publication that discusses cases where others filing for bankruptcy have dealt with this issue and a whole lot more

QUESTION: How far in advance is a good time to begin Pre-Planning my bankruptcy?

ANSWER: As soon as you know you might be filing for bankruptcy is the best time to begin laying out your plans.

You will want to have the info available to decide first of all if bankruptcy is the best

option you have for dealing with your financial situation.

If you conclude that YES filing for Chapter 7 or Chapter 13 Bankruptcy is your best solution then you would be wise to plan on about a SIX MONTH Pre Planning window.

If you think you cannot wait that long PLEASE think again and ask yourself if you can afford not to wait!

Before you begin making your plans please review my "Bankruptcy Control System" so that you are sure to control the Bankruptcy Filing Process from beginning to end.

You will find the "Bankruptcy Control System" outlined in detail in my now released "Everything" publication found on the home page.

QUESTION: How can i postpone filing bankruptcy with so many creditors and collection agencies breathing down my neck?

ANSWER: Well, there are a number of ways you can delay your filing but the one I recommend most involves your signing up with a local Consumer Credit Counseling Service (CCCS).

The number one reason I recommend signing with CCCS is that by doing so your behavior will more than likely be seen by the Bankruptcy Court as a legitimate attempt on your part to try and deal with your debt issues in a responsible manner.

In other words signing with CCCS will make you look good to the bankruptcy court.

The second reason is that CCCS is financed by the Credit Industry so they usually get their cooperation which means they can get these same eager creditors off of your back.

Also, you will have a good bankruptcy preparatory experience dealing with CCCS where you will have a good opportunity to sharpen your negotiation skills.

CCCS will be working with you on the amount of your plan payment so you will be required to supply them with income and expense figures.

You will need to negotiate expense figures you are willing to agree to in order to help determine the amount of your plan payment.

This is all part of the information you will need for the "Bankruptcy Control System" outlined in Ultimate Bankruptcy 2010".

Remember; Practice Makes Perfect - Right?

QUESTION: Is one bankruptcy chapter less detrimental to one's credit than another?

ANSWER: The answer to this question is kind of convoluted in that it seems just the opposite of what you might believe. If the level of your credit rating is a key area of importance to you when filing bankruptcy then Chapter 7 is definitely the chapter you want to file under!

Why? Well if you file a Chapter 13 bankruptcy you are going to be involved in a payment program that will last from (3) to (5) years!

What that means is that if you plan on repairing your credit score after filing bankruptcy … you will not be able to re-establish your credit for about 5 ½ years from the date of filing!

On the other hand if you file Chapter 7 Bankruptcy then you can begin repairing your credit just one month after Bankruptcy discharge … or around 3 months at the most after initially starting your bankruptcy process.

Why? Chapter 13 is a plan payment that lasts at least (3) years and today typically (5) years!

Chapter 7 Bankruptcy is a total discharge of all debt and is over once you have had your hearing and receive your discharge which occurs around one month after the hearing.

QUESTION: If i am in a Chapter 13 Bankruptcy where my Plan includes my auto lease payments and for whatever reason my case gets dismissed then what will happen to my car?

ANSWER: The real question you need to be asking is just how much time will you have before the leasing company repossess your vehicle?

if your vehicle has been forced into the plan then the lease payments have more than likely only been partial for the entire term of the plan up to the date of the court dismissal!

In order to save your car you will need to get an agreement with the leasing company.

You will no doubt need to bring your lease current by paying the leasing company a one time payment. Remember to have all details agreed to in writing in advance and signed by an authorized representative of the lease company.

If you can get their assistance have your Bankruptcy Attorney assist you with this matter.

I do not recommend any form of discussion with the leasing company until you have in hand the entire amount of money that is currently past due!

Remember that we are in the electronic age and so if your lease is through one of the large leasing companies like Honda Credit or one of the other big boys you may only have a couple of days!

I know of one case where the attorney did not bother to call or e-mail their client to warn them of their case dismissal and before notice had arrived in the mail their car had already been towed away!

This happened in a matter of only a few days. (2 - 3 days)

So what if this happens to you and you still have possession of your auto?

Well i have known of more than a few cases where the potential victim of this kind of aggressive tactic has simply stored their car in the garage of a friend until they were able to deal with the situation effectively.

What do i mean by effectively?

Until the person was able to either find a replacement auto or to borrow or save up enough money to bring their existing auto lease/loan current.

In this way they made certain not be left without transportation for work and were not forced to sacrifice their employment (means of survival) in any way.

QUESTION: Can I load my withholdings from my paycheck with exemption related items like optional profit-sharing deductions, maxed out 401K deductions, maxed out optional retirement funds, maxed out health benefits and any other options I can find to lower my take home income so that I can qualify for Chapter 7 bankruptcy over chapter 13?

ANSWER: Well sure, you can try just about anything you want to but please do not be surprised if the Bankruptcy Trustee forces you to remove all non-mandatory deductions!

If this happens and the Trustee does make such a requirement then just be aware you are exposed … and it will be very difficult to come up with an explanation for adding other expenses or income losses once you have shown your hand in the bankruptcy process.

It is always better to pre-plan and work with an attorney so that this sort of thing never happens with your case. There is really no good reason to gamble with this matter because a Chapter 13 Bankruptcy (5) year payment plan can be very expensive and very hard on you and your entire family.

QUESTION: Can IRS Debt be discharged through the bankruptcy process?

ANSWER: YES … but … There are certain rules that apply but the main one for past due income tax is that the IRS Debt must have been owed at least 3 years prior to the filing of bankruptcy. Secondly, the debt must be income tax related and not related to payroll taxes or other non-standard taxes.

As with all key questions related to the bankruptcy process PLEASE DISCUSS THESE MATTERS WITH YOUR BANKRUPTCY ATTORNEY! Only a reputable attorney is qualified to answer this and all questions that are legal in nature.

QUESTION: Do I actually need a "Bankruptcy Attorney" in order to get accurate information regarding bankruptcy law and procedure or for filing my bankruptcy case or will any practicing Attorney be ok?

ANSWER: If you are in need of a heart transplant would it be ok to use a general intern who is not a surgeon?

Law is filled with many specialized areas and disciplines and each one has its own set of special requirements. If you look in your yellow pages or on line you will see that most law offices specialize in key areas.

I feel that the best Bankruptcy Attorney is the one who works entirely in the bankruptcy arena and knows his practice and how the local trustee makes decisions based upon their interpretation of the bankruptcy law!

Personally I would never recommend going to a general practice law office unless that law firm has a special staff of attorneys who practice bankruptcy and nothing else and would have the experience and expertise to handle my case flawlessly.

If I were a heavy hitter and had a large amount of capital or assets and could afford it I would go to the law office where one of the trustee's actually practices and hire that trustee as my Bankruptcy Attorney.

Why?

No trustee is going to hassle another trustee because, in fact, they are all part of a social club that kind of watches each others back and is supportive in many ways.

Plus, who is going to know more about bankruptcy law and what is and is not acceptable more than one of the persons who over see's it all?

ALSO: Be certain that the attorney you end up retaining is available to you when you call on them!

Any attorney who does not return telephone calls in a timely manner or avoids talking with their clients is not the attorney who I want working for me!

Word of mouth may very well be your best form of referral.

Also, beware of "Attorney Referral Services" who are often set up by local Attorney's as a source for acquiring new client referrals!

If that is the case then you are only being referred to an attorney by a single attorney or group of attorneys who run the referral service in order to get new clients.

WORD OF MOUTH MAY BE YOUR VERY BEST BET ... IF YOU CAN GET IT.

Also, be sure you know why they like who they are recommending.

An Attorney conducting Friendly discussions about their latest time on the golf course or "that 49'ers game" is not a good reason to retain an attorney.

U.S. Bankruptcy Court Resource Guide

(The Following are U.S. Bankruptcy Court Video's – Documents – Forms.)

"MEANS TEST" Forms

Chapter 7 Statement of Current Income & Means Test Form 22A

http://www.uscourts.gov/rules/BK_Forms_08_Official/B_022A_1208.pdf

Chapter 13 Means Test Statement of Income (Commitment Period-Disposable Income)

http://www.uscourts.gov/rules/BK_Forms_08_Official/B_022C_0108v2.pdf

INTRODUCTION to Bankruptcy   (VIDEO'S - U.S. BK Court)

http://tinyurl.com/6fnft5

BASICS - From U.S. Bankruptcy Court Archive

http://www.uscourts.gov/bankruptcycourts/bankbasics.pdf

FORMS - ALL (Current Forms from - U.S. Bankruptcy Court Archive)

http://www.uscourts.gov/bkforms/bankruptcy_forms.html#official

GLOSSARY - From U.S. Bankruptcy Court Archive

http://www.uscourts.gov/bankruptcycourts/bankruptcybasics/glossary.html

FILING PROCESS - From U.S. Bankruptcy Court Archive

http://www.uscourts.gov/bankruptcycourts/bankruptcybasics/process.html

DISCHARGE in Bankruptcy: **Archive from U.S. Bankruptcy Court**

http://www.uscourts.gov/bankruptcycourts/bankruptcybasics/discharge.html

BANKRUPTCY CRIME – PAY CLOSE ATTENTION TO THIS VIDEO!

http://tinyurl.com/ybxovtx

Note: Even though this video is in the general mix I wanted to single it out so that you do not over look what is being said here! I only recommend complete honesty in your bankruptcy filing process! I never recommend that you lie or withhold any information related to your bankruptcy case or break any
of the laws related to filing for bankruptcy!

Help is On The Way: (Taking the Pressure Off)

http://www.usdoj.gov/ust/eo/bapcpa/ccde/index.htm

Frequently Asked Questions – U.S. Bankruptcy Trustee

http://www.usdoj.gov/ust/eo/bapcpa/trustees_faqs.htm#ch13_issue

U.S. Bankruptcy Court Locations Nationwide

PLEASE NOTE: This Book Includes a FREE Active Link PDF E-Book Version. Click Here to Download Your Copy:

http://tinyurl.com/yye4xkn

Simply click on all colored/underlined text to be taken to the location being linked.

List of All On-line U.S. Bankruptcy Court Websites (just click on listing)

Alabama Middle Bankruptcy Court

Alabama Northern Bankruptcy Court

Alabama Southern Bankruptcy Court

Alaska Bankruptcy Court

Arizona Bankruptcy Court

Arkansas Eastern Bankruptcy Court

Arkansas Western Bankruptcy Court

California Central Bankruptcy Court

California Eastern Bankruptcy Court

California Northern Bankruptcy Court

California Southern Bankruptcy Court

Colorado Bankruptcy Court

Connecticut Bankruptcy Court

DC Bankruptcy Court

Delaware Bankruptcy Court

Florida Middle Bankruptcy Court

Florida Northern Bankruptcy Court

Florida Southern Bankruptcy Court

Georgia Middle Bankruptcy Court

Georgia Northern Bankruptcy Court

Georgia Southern Bankruptcy Court

Guam Bankruptcy Court

Hawaii Bankruptcy Court

Idaho Bankruptcy Court

Online Illinois Central Bankruptcy Court

Illinois Northern Bankruptcy Court

Illinois Southern Bankruptcy Court

Indiana Northern Bankruptcy Court

Indiana Southern Bankruptcy Court

Iowa Northern Bankruptcy Court

Iowa Southern Bankruptcy Court

Kansas Bankruptcy Court

Kentucky Eastern Bankruptcy Court

Kentucky Western Bankruptcy Court

Louisiana Eastern Bankruptcy Court

Louisiana Middle Bankruptcy Court

Louisiana Western Bankruptcy Court

Maine Bankruptcy Court

Maryland Bankruptcy Court

Massachusetts Bankruptcy Court

Michigan Eastern Bankruptcy Court

Michigan Western Bankruptcy Court

Minnesota Bankruptcy Court

Mississippi Northern Bankruptcy Court

Mississippi Southern Bankruptcy Court

Missouri Eastern Bankruptcy Court

Missouri Western Bankruptcy Court

Montana Bankruptcy Court

Nebraska Bankruptcy Court

Nevada Bankruptcy Court

New Hampshire Bankruptcy Court

New Jersey Bankruptcy Court

New Mexico Bankruptcy Court

New York Eastern Bankruptcy Court

New York Northern Bankruptcy Court

New York Southern Bankruptcy Court

New York Western Bankruptcy Court

North Carolina Eastern Bankruptcy Court

North Carolina Middle Bankruptcy Court

North Carolina Western Bankruptcy Court

North Dakota Bankruptcy Court

Ohio Northern Bankruptcy Court

Ohio Southern Bankruptcy Court

Oklahoma Eastern Bankruptcy Court

Oklahoma Northern Bankruptcy Court

Oklahoma Western Bankruptcy Court

Oregon Bankruptcy Court

Pennsylvania Eastern Bankruptcy Court

Pennsylvania Middle Bankruptcy Court

Pennsylvania Western Bankruptcy Court

Puerto Rico Bankruptcy Court

Rhode Island Bankruptcy Court

South Carolina Bankruptcy Court

South Dakota Bankruptcy Court

Tennessee Eastern Bankruptcy Court

Tennessee Middle Bankruptcy Court

Tennessee Western Bankruptcy Court

Texas Eastern Bankruptcy

Texas Northern Bankruptcy Court

Texas Southern Bankruptcy Court

Texas Western Bankruptcy Court

Utah Bankruptcy Court

Vermont Bankruptcy Court

Virginia Eastern Bankruptcy Court

Virginia Western Bankruptcy Court

Virgin Islands Bankruptcy Court

Washington Eastern Bankruptcy Court

Washington Western Bankruptcy Court

West Virginia Northern Bankruptcy Court

West Virginia Southern Bankruptcy Court

Wisconsin Eastern Bankruptcy Court

Wisconsin Western Bankruptcy

Wyoming Bankruptcy Court

USE OF WORK SHEETS AND FORMS

The work sheets included in the following section have all been re-created as MS Word Docs and are available at the link below:

http://tinyurl.com/yye4xkn

Because they are in MS Word Format they can easily be edited by you and printed as your personal worksheets.

Please go through each of these work sheets and remove any item that is not relevant to your particular situation.

Please only make changes to these work sheets after you have been to at least (1) of your Free Bankruptcy Consultations.

Then Refine these sets following each of the remaining Free Bankruptcy Consultations.

Bankruptcy Work List - PRINT

Total Amount of Unsecured Debt $ _____
(credit cards, store charges, gas cards, casino credit accounts, etc)

Total Number of Unsecured Creditors   _____

Total Amount of Secured Debt $ _____
(Including: home mortgages, auto loans/leases, boat loans, furniture store accounts, home electronics, major appliances, etc)

Total Number of Secured Creditors   _____

Number of Homes/Real Estate Owned   _____

Primary Residence Value $ _____

Amount of Mortgage $_____

Combined Value-all other Real Estate $ _____

Combined Amount of these RE Loans $ _____

Number of Vehicles Owned   _____

Value of Main Vehicle Owned $ _____

Amount of Loan on Main Vehicle $ _____

Number of Other Vehicles Owned   _____

Value for All Other Vehicles Owned $ _____

Total Owed for All Other Vehicles $ _____

Number of RV's Owned   _____
Including: Boats, Motorhomes, Mobilehomes, Motorcycles, Dirt Bikes, Gliders, Jet Ski's, etc

Total Value for All RV's Owned $ _____

    104

Total Amount Owed on All RV's $ _____

Total Amount of IRS/Govrment Debt $ _____
(IRS Debt Owed for (3) Years or Less)

Total Debt Created in past 90 Days $ _____

Sub-Totals – Assets & Indebtedness

INDEBTEDNESS:

Total Amount Non-Dischargeable Debt $ _____
(Including: Child Support, Spousal Support, School Loans, DUI Related Debt, etc)

Total Amount of Dischargeable Debt $ _____
(including: Credit Card, Store Charge, Medical & Dental Bills, Hospital Bills, etc)

Total Amount of Secured Debt $ _____
(Real Estate, Automobiles, RV's, Major Electronics, Furnishings, etc)

ASSETS:

Total Combined Family Income (net) $ _____

Total Value of all Property Owned $ _____

Total Value Contracts/Partnrships, etc $ _____

Bankruptcy Checklist - PRINT

(Print out and use this checklist as you complete
each element of your bankruptcy)

ITEMS THAT NEED TO BE COMPLETED **AT LEAST SIX MONTHS
PRIOR TO FILING BANKRUPTCY** (Anything less Than Four Months Is
asking for serious trouble you do not need!)

____ Complete "**General Bankruptcy Work List**" (last page of this
publication)

____ Complete **First of Three Free Consultations** with a local
Bankruptcy Attorney (a minimum of (3) consultations needed)

____ Complete answers to the **"Critical Questions"** List (next page
following this checklist) including questions you add for your
particular situation (Bring the latest updated copy to each Free
Bankruptcy Consultation)

____ Complete **Median Income Evaluation** for the state where you
reside and plan to file. (see Page 67 of this publication)

____ Complete "**Means Test**" to see where you stand.(see Page 67 of
this Publication) (bring results to all remaining bankruptcy
consultations)

____ Complete **List of Creditors** of all people you owe money to and be
Certain to include EVERYONE you owe money too including
friends and Family alike!

____ Complete my **List of Assets** for all property that you own or have
interest in. (enter information into "**General Bankruptcy Work
List**" found on last page of this publication)

____ Complete my next two (or more) Free Bankruptcy Consultations
with Local Bankruptcy Attorneys. Be sure to ask any questions you
have Regarding any of the above completed items you will be

bringing with you to each of your remaining Bankruptcy Consultations

____ Determine what Bankruptcy Attorney to Retain and discuss and/or negotiate the cost for their service plus any other related fees (such as Bankruptcy Court Filing Fee or other legal fees).

____ Set aside funds needed for Bankruptcy Attorney Fee Plus Bankruptcy Court Filing Fee (based upon info from free bankruptcy consultations.)

____ Determine Best Date to file bankruptcy according to my particular situation and based upon results of my Bankruptcy Control Plan and taking into account all elements of my situation.

(Remember to take all key factors into account for maximizing my results and guaranteeing that I am able to file under the Bankruptcy Chapter that **I determine is best for Me (and not for the banks and creditors)**

____ Make any plans regarding employment (for self or spouse) in order to acquire the Bankruptcy Chapter that serves my needs best.

____ Sign up with a Consumer Credit Counseling Services Program (if that is needed to keep creditors off of my back)

____ Purchase/Lease any vehicle that you plan to use following the filing of my Bankruptcy.

____ Purchase Real Property if filing Chapter 13 (if My Bankruptcy Plan calls for such a purchase)

____ Pay off any creditors that you do not want to file bankruptcy on (doctors you want to keep, services you don't' want to loose, etc)

____ Convert any non-dischargeable debt into dischargeable debt by paying one off with the other (i.e. Credit Card cash advances to pay off school loans)

____ Transfer any properties you plan to change ownership on.

____ Have name removed from any will or debts currently owed to you.

____ Cash out all checks/notes/payments for property currently owed by you.

FINAL ITEMS THAT NEED TO BE DONE A FEW WEEKS PRIOR TO ACTUALLY FILING MY BANKRUPTCY:

____ Determine date for Paying Partial or Full Retainer Fee to Bankruptcy Attorney (this needs to be done a few weeks prior to actual filing the Bankruptcy Petition.)

____ Pay my Bankruptcy Attorney agreed upon Retainer Fee plus Bankruptcy Court Filing Fee.

____ Bring single copy of each of my most current billing statements.

____ Make certain that my list of Creditors (including all debts that have been transferred to Collection Agencies) are included on my final list. Be sure to include EVERYONE you owe money to!

____ Locate then Visit Hearing Location a week or so prior to actual hearing date.

____ Contact Bankruptcy Attorney for final briefing on hearing and make certain that you have all items needed at hearing available to me and ready! (Bring list of any additional creditors I have discovered since turning info over to the bankruptcy attorney/staff.

____ Bring list of any final questions you have regarding my bankruptcy and the Meeting of Creditors Hearing.

____ Order my copy of "How to Have Your Good Credit Back Just Six Months after Bankruptcy"

____ Tax returns for the previous (2) years

____ Previous (2) Months of Paycheck Stubs (copies in some cases for example you are paid by direct deposit only)

Critical Questions List - PRINT

This is a General List of Questions that need to be asked during your Free Bankruptcy Consultations with a qualified Bankruptcy Attorney.

Go through this list and only leave questions that are relevant to your own particular situation and remove those that are not. ADD any questions not found here that are relevant to your own particular needs. PRINT OUT THIS FORM AND USE DURING YOUR FREE CONSULTATIONS.

- What Chapter of Bankruptcy can I file with my current financial situation?
- How does the "Means Test" affect my bankruptcy filing? (see forms on page 69 of this publication)
- Is the "State Median Income" amount based on gross income (before taxes & withholding) or net income (after taxes & withholding)?
- Can I keep (or surrender) my house?
- Will I have to pay any of my debts once I have filed?
- What about my IRS debt?
- What about my School Loan Debt?
- Can I keep my Cars?
- What about my Car Payments?
- Can I keep my Retirement?
- Can I prevent Wage Garnishment?
- Can I prevent Liens on my property?
- What if I have a lien on my property will It be removed?
- Can I keep my Personal Collections (coins, guns, antiques, jewelry)?
- Can I keep my Boat, RV, Trailer, etc?

- What Happens to payments on Boat, RV, Trailer, etc?
- Can I keep my tools that I use for my work?
- What about future money/property that I may receive in wills from family members?
- Can I keep my interest in my business partnership?
- What about property that belongs to a business/partnership I am involved with?
- What happens to child support payments I owe?
- What happens to spousal support payments I owe?
- What happens with hospital bills that I owe?
- What happens with medical bills that I owe?
- What happens if I want to pay a particular family doctor in order to keep their services for my child or other family member?
- What happens to an ambulance bill I have with the county?
- What about debts I have with my dentist?
- Can I pay back money I owe to family members/friends prior to filing my bankruptcy?
- What happens to a car where the loan/title is listed in my name but all payments have been made by son / daughter / friend and the vehicle actually belongs to them? (I just took out the loan for them)
- Can I keep my life insurance plan?
- Can I keep my health insurance plan?
- What happens to my 401K and Retirement/Pension Accounts?
- What exactly is the "Means Test" and how will it affect my bankruptcy filing?
- How will my spouses Social Security Income affect my means test income?
- What happens to my accounts that have been turned over to collection agencies?

- How will the bankruptcy rules affect me and my wife since we are now living separately but still married?
- What happens if my spouse is filing for bankruptcy on debts that were owed prior to our marriage?
- What kind of income deductions will the bankruptcy trustee allow me to continue making that are related to my retirement/health insurance/profit sharing?

_____

_____

_____

_____

_____

_____

_____

_____

_____

_____

www.ingramcontent.com/pod-product-compliance
Lightning Source LLC
Chambersburg PA
CBHW081134170526
45165CB00008B/2673